COACHING
THE STREETS

COACHING
THE STREETS
Richard "Digger" Phelps
with Jack Colwell

COACHING THE STREETS

Cover photo credit: South Bend Tribune /Greg Swiercz

10 9 8 7 6 5 4 3 2

Library of Congress Contro: Number: 2013944171
ISBN 978-0-9890731-2-7

Distributed by ACTA Publications
4848 N. Clark Street, Chicago, IL 60640.
800-397-2282, www.actapublications.com

Published by
CORBY BOOKS
A Division of Corby Publishing, LP
P.O. Box 93
Notre Dame, IN 46556
11961 Tyler Road
Lakeville, IN 46536
Editorial Office: (574) 784-3482

Manufactured in the United States of America

TO SUE SHIDLER
Who inspired me to write this book.

Sue was assistant director
of the Notre Dame Bookstore.
She loved Notre Dame and gave her all
to provide a warm and friendly atmosphere
for campus visitors.
She was a great friend
and urged me to write about
coaching the streets,
a cause she supported,
even as she waged
her own battle against cancer.

Died April 22, 2013

Sue will be missed by all who knew and loved her.

CONTENTS

CHAPTER ONE

Shocked by Shootings
"Youth Violence Spike".. 1

CHAPTER TWO

Father Ted's Challenge
"That's It?"..11

CHAPTER THREE

Challenging Kids
Not "Dumb-dumbs"..21

CHAPTER FOUR

NRA's Way
"Gin Up Fears." ....,..29

CHAPTER FIVE

Music City
"You HAVE Overcome."...............................39

CHAPTER SIX

After Katrina
"Walking to New Orleans"...........................45

CHAPTER SEVEN

Culinary School
"Was a Sorry Mess".. 55

CHAPTER EIGHT

Columnist's Opinion
"Speaks from the Heart"... 61

CHAPTER NINE

A Plan
With a "BAM"... 69

CHAPTER TEN

Disrespect
"I'm Shootin' Your Ass Off."..................................... 77

CHAPTER ELEVEN

Respect
"Let's Figure This Out."...89

CHAPTER TWELVE

What Parents?
"Raised on the Streets"...99

CHAPTER THIRTEEN

Finding Hooks
"You Can Save a Thousand."......................................107

CHAPTER FOURTEEN

Funny Thing
"Not How You Throw a Chair"...................................117

CHAPTER FIFTEEN

Brazen Gangs
"Counterinsurgency Tactics"......................................125

CHAPTER SIXTEEN

Medical Magnet
And a "Crossing"...131

CHAPTER SEVENTEEN

Dream Team Mentors
And Students "Giving Back"..141

CHAPTER EIGHTEEN

The Motto
"Don't Assume It Can't Be Done."..............................147

CHAPTER NINETEEN

Boston Strong
"Isn't the Reaction That Terrorists Want"...................155

CHAPTER TWENTY

New Opponent
"Have the Courage."...165

A Smorgasbord 171

CHAPTER ONE

Shocked by Shootings
"Youth Violence Spike"

COACHING THE STREETS, as I do now, is a lot like coaching basketball, as I did for 20 seasons at the University of Notre Dame. You still need a game plan. Still have to recruit players. Still must search for a starting lineup with leadership. Still need a lot of other willing players to take key roles. And it still requires hard work and teamwork to win. The biggest difference is that the streets can be deadly. If a player loses there, it's a life, not just a game, which ends.

I'm no stranger to the realities of violence in our streets. When I left coaching at Notre Dame, I ran Operation Weed and Seed in the administration of President George H.W. Bush. That was a coordinated effort to weed out the drug dealers and gangs in some of the most violent, crime-ridden neighborhoods in the nation and then seed those areas with programs to provide economic opportunities and

1

positive choices for kids. So I saw the worst. I'm not shocked by much.

But I was shocked by a newspaper story I read when I returned to my South Bend home after the 2012 NCAA Final Four. Hey, season's over. Now, a little respite from my gig as an ESPN basketball analyst, I thought. Then I picked up the paper. And there would be no respite. Not after I saw on April 10 a front-page story in the *South Bend Tribune* with this headline: "City sees youth violence spike."

The story told of five young people being shot in three violent incidents. One 16-year-old boy died after a drive-by shooting in which another teen was wounded and a third escaped the flying bullets from a passing car. An 18-year-old was shot by an assailant who jumped out of a car to fire away. And then, at an informal prom called "Swagger Fest" at the downtown Century Center, a gunman—or two, according to some reports—jumped onstage and fired into the crowd. A 17-year-old female and a 20-year-old male were wounded. In earlier incidents, the story related, three teenagers were killed by gunfire.

Whoa!

This was not Chicago, New York or Los Angeles. This was not one of those notorious urban areas of violence we focused on with Weed and Seed. This was in South Bend, Indiana, my town, where I have promoted mentoring and after-school programs to keep kids off the streets and out of trouble. And now streets not that far from my own home, not that far from the Notre Dame campus, were becoming as violent as the Chicago streets where gang warfare rages.

Something was really wrong. Something had to be done.

Inspired still by the challenge I had received years before from Father Ted Hesburgh, the great former president of the University of Notre Dame, I knew I had to act—to coach in those streets. The challenge was to go beyond the comfortable life of TV basketball analyst and make a moral commitment to God and to Notre Dame to try to make things better for others—to make a difference.

I've been trying—sponsoring, encouraging and pushing local efforts for mentoring; providing backpacks with school supplies for children who otherwise would start school without them; and fixing up older, rundown schools to make them more inviting for kids for study and after-school programs.

This new type of coaching in places other than Notre Dame's Joyce Center has taken me to New Orleans, a city I love and know well from my days of successful recruiting there. After the heartbreaking devastation from Hurricane Katrina, I sponsored the construction of new homes for deserving folks afflicted by the storm, and pleaded and cajoled successfully for turning McDonogh High School (with

3

its warped floors and leaking ceilings from the storm) into a school with culinary training for jobs in the city's great restaurants.

And, in Memphis, I helped to promote and raise funds for Soulsville Stax Music Academy Charter School, located in a troubled area. This school also is designed for interests and opportunities in its city. In addition to offering challenging basic courses, Soulsville provides training in music in the Music City. I was honored to be one of the commencement speakers there in 2012 for the first graduating class—and proud that all 51 graduates had been accepted for college.

Well, if we can have success in New Orleans and Memphis, why can't we have projects like that all over the country? Now, specifically, I thought, why can't we field a team for a project to stem the violence right at home, right in South Bend?

I went to work, recruiting.

On the phone all day for days, I sought players for a "Stop Youth Violence Team." I called and often went to visit public officials, educators, police officials, bankers, business executives, union leaders, members of the clergy, social services representatives and others that I knew or knew of as having the expertise to help.

"I'll coach it," I told them. "But I need your help."
Almost all, shocked also by the violence, said "yes."

My starting five were ready: The mayor, the

school superintendent, the chief of police, the city council president and an important fifth player that is not one single person—the news media.

South Bend Mayor Pete Buttigieg is a new, young leader, elected mayor at age 29 in 2011. Some citizens still have difficulty with the pronunciation of his name, but I don't see what's so hard about pronouncing "Pete." He gets it. He is a star player with efforts to curb violence and improve conditions through economic development and removal of vacant houses in areas where crime breeds.

School Superintendent Carole Schmidt is a strong proponent of mentoring, tutoring, and providing after-school programs.

Police Chief Chuck Hurley, serving then as an interim chief, encouraged our efforts and strove to keep internal police disputes over removal of the prior chief from hindering a robust response to the violence.

Council President Derek Dieter, who also is a policeman, joined immediately to help our efforts through both his council leadership and his police training and experience.

The news media played a vital role. We needed coverage, broadcast and print, to get out the message about the extent and danger of this violence and about our efforts to curb it and seek cures. We didn't expect all positive coverage. And there were stories about some disputes, political jealousies and

5

differing opinions on how to cope with the problem. That's fine. There is no team that never loses or that never is the subject of a negative story. The worst blow is no story at all—an indication that nobody cares.

We packed the Kroc Center auditorium with a crowd of nearly 700 concerned folks for a "Town Hall Meeting to Stop Youth Violence." The need to act was punctuated by more gunfire. Four more young people were shot in two incidents just up the street from the center on the weekend before the meeting. Two died.

Our goals presented at the meeting were: (1) to recruit 500 additional mentors for at-risk children; (2) to expand after-school programs; and (3) to promote community policing that would feature cooperation of neighborhood-watch teams and police.

By "neighborhood watch," I'm NOT talking about the type of "watch" that led to the fatal shooting of Trayvon Martin, an unarmed 17-year-old, in Florida. That was not the community policing I advocate. I want neighborhood-watch volunteers who wouldn't carry guns or try to enforce the law themselves. They wouldn't, in most cases, even call police to make arrests. They would watch for signs of trouble and then give the police information to prevent crime, not just make arrests after violence.

Watch volunteers, to be effective rather than simply cause resentment, must reflect the makeup of the neighborhood. A bunch of white volunteers, though well-meaning, isn't likely to communicate effectively with black kids in a black neighborhood. Communication is essential in learning what's happening and who needs help.

For example, during Weed and Seed, our projects weren't working well in some Hispanic neighborhoods. I found one reason was that there were no Hispanic community police officers, no officers who looked like, talked like or understood the folks there.

Why? I was given the excuse that Hispanics couldn't pass the police tests.

"Then change the tests," I demanded. If none of the intelligent and capable Hispanics in the entire area could pass the tests, there was something wrong with the questions or evaluation of the answers.

Not everybody was immediately enthusiastic about our South Bend efforts to curb the violence. For example, the president of "Mamas Against Violence," whose own son had been shot and killed, told a reporter at the town hall meeting that mentoring programs are nothing new. "We have these mentor programs and normally they're short term," she said. "You mentor kids for six months, a year, and then what happens to that kid?" She was right—but also wrong if she thought mentoring was always a waste. Mentoring is no panacea. All mentors are not created equal. Some, though trying, may not reach a troubled child. Not every troubled child will respond to even the most dedicated mentor. And just a little mentoring, with no additional help or guidance afterward, may be useless. However, here we find another similarity with coaching on the basketball court. In basketball, every shot for a three-pointer won't be successful. In mentoring, every attempt won't make a difference. That doesn't mean that a basketball team, after missing several shots, should never try for a three-pointer to win a game. And if some mentoring attempts don't seem to be successful, that doesn't mean there should be no further try to hit a winning shot with a kid who will respond.

I have heard so many stories about how a mentor helped to change the life of a kid in a positive way—real success stories. Mentoring is worthwhile. With an additional 500 mentors, how many success stories could there be? I don't know. Even though there won't be 100 percent success, any percentage of success is far better than no success at all.

The most vehement and surprising opposition to our efforts against violence came from two city council members. The vehemence apparently stemmed from politics and personal squabbles. You know, kind of like Congress. They were opposed politically and personally to the mayor and police chief on other matters and apparently had no desire to join in an effort those officials supported.

Their opposition was surprising—and terribly disappointing—because both of these council members are African-Americans. Victims of this terrible violence were, in most cases, African-American kids. I was surprised also because of my lifelong positive relationships—from being the only white kid in Beacon, New York, playing basketball with black friends on the most challenging courts, to the successful recruiting of black players at Notre Dame, to my efforts in New Orleans and Memphis.

But my call for each council member to help to recruit neighborhood-watch teams brought an angry outburst from one of the councilmen who complained that proper protocol was for the request to come from the mayor or through a measure sponsored by a council member. (Actually, the call was also from the mayor and the council president.) Offense was taken, I guess, when I challenged the council politicians: "You knocked on houses for votes. I'm asking you to knock on houses for support of neighborhood watch."

The other council member who bashed our efforts bristled when I interjected comments in support of South Bend schools. "You are out of order," he declared, saying that what I might argue on a basketball court couldn't be tolerated under council parliamentary rules.

Was I out of order in parliamentary procedure for commenting when I did? Probably. "Give me a technical," I said. I probably deserved one—just as I did at times during basketball games. Sometimes a coach needs to take a technical, to make a point with the refs, to stir up the home crowd or to divert an away-crowd's hostility toward the coach and away from the team.

Anyway, I just didn't care about protocol or politics when we have kids killing each other.

Did we stop all the shooting? Of course not. We did, however, see months without fatal violence. Coincidence? No, I think we helped. A factor certainly was knowledge in the streets that "the heat's on." Heat. Cold. Whatever it takes. If we saved a few lives, I'll take that. And if we can get more programs in place to turn around lives, to save lives in the future, I'll crusade for that.

CHAPTER TWO

Father Ted's Challenge
"That's It?"

FATHER TED, KNOWN FORMALLY as the Rev. Theodore M. Hesburgh, C.S.C., is known to me as an inspiration and a friend. He can be very persuasive. In fact, Father Ted is the reason I coach the streets today rather than returning home from a season of basketball analysis on ESPN to take it easy, play golf, do some painting in Europe and let the at-risk kids in the streets take care of themselves.

This great man, who attained stature and respect in government as well as in religion and education, was president of Notre Dame from 1952 to 1987, a time of academic excellence, the admission of female students and continued athletic renown. He was the man with the final say when I was hired as Notre Dame's head basketball coach back in 1971 at age 29. Ever since then, he has been supportive, concerned about my welfare, and concerned as well that I do my best to help others to set and achieve goals in their lives.

We didn't want to disappoint Father Ted with our performance on the court or —just as important—with the performance of the players in the classroom. I'm proud of averaging nearly 20 wins a year and pulling upsets over seven No. 1-ranked teams during my two decades as coach at Notre Dame. I'm prouder still of a 100-percent graduation rate—what Father Ted wanted, and expected, during those 20 years.

Father Ted's influence extended well beyond the campus. Without his persuasive efforts on the Civil Rights Commission, to which he was appointed by President Eisenhower in 1957, there would not have been the progress that led to passage of the historic Civil Rights Act of 1964.

President Barack Obama accepted Notre Dame's invitation to be the 2009 Commencement speaker in order to honor Father Hesburgh for his dedicated efforts and achievements on civil rights. From the days not really that long ago when an African-American in parts of our nation couldn't sit at a lunch counter or in the front of the bus, we have progressed to where an African-American had the opportunity to run for president, win and sit in the Oval Office.

While some critics of Obama's policies sought to politicize the Commencement, Father Ted was there to hear, appreciate and acknowledge the President's tribute. Hesburgh had furthered a tradition of inviting presidents and presidential candidates to speak at Notre Dame, no matter their views. And he was pleased that the graduates silenced the few planted hecklers in the audience with the loud, proud shout from football: "We are ND!"

Yes, they were. The hecklers were not. And Obama delivered his tribute to the persuasive efforts of Hesburgh back when a diverse Civil Rights Commission—including Southern governors and the dean of a Southern law school—was deadlocked after two years of work and could not even meet together at hotels and restaurants in the South because one member was an African-American.

The President related the story of Hesburgh's persuasive persistence with the commission: "Finally when they reached an impasse in Louisiana, Father Ted flew them all to Notre Dame's retreat in Land O'Lakes, Wisconsin, where they eventually overcame their differences and hammered out a final deal."

The President recalled Father Ted's story of how he discovered that the members were all fishermen and, thus, arranged a twilight boat trip on the lake. "They fished, and they talked, and they changed the course of history," Obama said.

Father Hesburgh's persuasion extends beyond this country. His was a voice of sanity in seeking to halt the Cold War nuclear arms race and ban nuclear testing that was poisoning the atmosphere.

He also was an inspirational and persuasive

13

figure in the life of José Napoleón Duarte, the first Notre Dame graduate to become a head of state. Duarte was president of El Salvador, becoming the first popularly elected civilian leader of his country in 50 years when he was elected amid civil war there in 1984.

When Duarte came to Notre Dame as a student in the 1940s, he didn't understand English. So, as a student in the religion class that Father Hesburgh was teaching at that time, he had a tough time figuring out what the priest was saying. Instead of waiting to seek clarification, he constantly disrupted the class, mumbling in Spanish while seeking a translation from other students.

An oft-told story is that Hesburgh finally brought Duarte to a classroom window and threatened to throw him out—out the window—if he didn't stop the disruption. Duarte and Hesburgh both confirmed that the story is true.

Though probably suspecting the priest was making a point rather than actually intending to send him head-first out the window, Duarte took no chances. He learned English quickly and became a more serious student, graduating in 1948 with a degree in civil engineering. Hesburgh and "Nappy," as he always fondly called his one-time window-brink student, built a lasting friendship.

Just as President Obama spoke to honor Hesburgh at a later Commencement, Duarte came as president of El Salvador to deliver the Notre Dame Commencement address in 1985. He told the graduates that it was a challenge from Hesburgh that led him on a quest for "freeing my country from the two totalitarian extremes—the Marxists and the fascists." Hesburgh persuaded him in that challenge in 1960 to make "a moral commitment to Notre Dame and a historical commitment to your country" and not just "stand with your arms folded."

And so the engineering graduate sought to engineer a path to democracy, a dangerous path through the violence and terror and death squads of the El Salvadoran civil war.

Duarte traversed that path to win the 1972 presidential election—sort of. The military stole the election from Duarte and, after torturing him, was planning to kill him.

"I am alive today," Duarte said in his Commencement speech, "only because Father Hesburgh interceded on my behalf before Pope Paul VI and the president of the United States, Richard Nixon."

Though his life was saved, Duarte was sent into exile for eight years. He continued to pursue that "moral commitment" in the Hesburgh challenge and finally won another presidential election—this time able to take office. He brought reforms but couldn't end the hostilities.

Supporters of the leftist side in those hostilities demonstrated against selection of Duarte as

Commencement speaker. A few negative signs were raised as he spoke. But just as was to happen again two dozen graduation ceremonies later, the graduates came through with what Hesburgh called some of the loudest applause he ever heard at Commencement.

It was in 1996 at a Notre Dame function when Father Ted challenged me to do more.

"So what have you been doing?" he asked. I told him about my work as an ESPN basketball analyst, a great gig, with all summer off for golf and travel, including doing some painting in Europe.

"That's it?" he asked. "No, what have you really been doing?"

I knew what he meant. What was I doing for what really matters? What was my moral commitment to help others, to try to make the world a little better place and not just observe with my arms folded?

"Don't give me the Duarte story," I joked.

But he had, of course. He had given me the challenge to do more. We had many times talked about education and how to improve opportunities for kids who fall through the cracks. In running Operation Weed and Seed for President George H.W. Bush after I left coaching at Notre Dame, I was aware of the problems on the streets—the drugs, the crime, the violence—and the need to keep kids in school and out of the streets. I already was involved in promoting mentoring and after-school programs. So that was an area where perhaps I could do more. But what?

16

The answer was right at home, in South Bend, where the school system, short on funding, had some older schools in less-affluent areas in desperate need of repair. Kids should have pride in their schools, not find them dingy places, dumps where they are dumped. Schools should provide an atmosphere conducive to learning. They should be places where students are welcome for after-school programs, especially at times when too many kids otherwise will be wandering the streets, getting in trouble. The danger times are from 3 to 5 p.m.

Lincoln Elementary School, on the city's southeast side, serving many families below the poverty line, was built in 1910 and needed renovation—really, really needed to be fixed up, brightened up and brought up to date.

That's where I would coach again. I recruited a team during a speech to the South Bend Rotary Club, challenging the members of the city's leading service club to take on a project of fixing up a school. They agreed.

I went to local businesses, seeking donations of supplies and equipment as well as funding. Businesses will help if they see a worthy cause and know their contributions will be used wisely, not wasted. Our goal of $175,000 was exceeded. We topped $200,000. Sherwin Williams, one of the big donors, provided $20,000 worth of paint and brushes.

We needed volunteers to do the work, some hard

17

work. And we needed a game plan for the massive effort, to be accomplished mainly in one day, but with follow-up work to complete some of the major projects.

In my earlier book, *Undertaker's Son*, I gave these details:

On June 20, 1998, a Saturday, more than seven hundred people showed up at Lincoln to paint walls, wash woodwork, rip out old carpet and blackboards, and prepare to affix replacements, install new ceiling tiles and lighting fixtures, polish railings, plant flowers and shrubbery, trim trees, and plan for after-school projects. Most of the work was done on that one frantic day, for which the sponsoring Rotarians had joined in organizing well, with specific instructions for paint colors for each room and with color-coded T-shirts for the crowd: yellow for security, black for leaders, aqua for Rotary members, white for school families, royal blue for skilled trades people, red for nurses.

We had great local news coverage, important for getting volunteers and attracting support for future school projects. We even drew national coverage on NBC's "The Today Show" and on ESPN.

The most important attention we attracted? It was from the kids attending Lincoln. The principal and teachers reported that the students took pride in their more attractive school. More than three hundred of them began participating in after-school programs— from stamp club to cooking class.

I was coaching again, the type of coaching Father Hesburgh meant when he challenged me to do more. We did more. We fixed up more schools. We attracted more mentors.

In this type of coaching, just as in basketball, I found the need to get on the officials.

A school superintendent announced plans to close Lincoln School. The school we did so much to rejuvenate in 1998 was to be abandoned by 2006. She suggested that Lincoln kids could be sent off to another school far to the south. That would hurt the Lincoln neighborhood, hurt the kids. It would kill the after-school programs in which two-thirds of the students were participating.

Time out! No way. I went to the school board, taking on the superintendent as I would a basketball ref who had blown calls and didn't seem to care. They did their version of calling technical fouls on me.

I didn't threaten to throw anybody out the window. But just as the young Duarte didn't know for sure if Father Hesburgh was serious about the window bit, the school officials didn't seem to know how to respond to me, especially when the public and the *South Bend Tribune* in a strong editorial agreed with me.

The board relented. They decided not to abandon the neighborhood. They would instead build a new school at the Lincoln site. They did. And it now is open.

My challenge was successful—just as Father Hesburgh's challenge to me was successful. He got me to coach the streets, to persist and not to be deterred when slapped with technical fouls from some school board or city council members.

CHAPTER THREE

Challenging Kids
Not "Dumb-dumbs"

KEEPING KIDS OFF dangerous streets and in school is essential in curbing violence and preparing this nation for the global competition that will determine our future economic growth and standard of living.

What, however, do we expect in our schools?

Too often, not much.

Not much for the kids written off as "remedial" and "warehoused" in high schools until they can drop out. Not much for young athletes, potential leaders, when they are allowed to glide through high school without academic challenge, without learning skills vital for their future.

In most Indiana high schools, a kid is eligible for football or basketball or other sports and extracurricular activities with five D's and an F. The requirement is just passing 70 percent of the classes. It doesn't matter if the 70 percent are passed with terrible D grades and the kid flat out flunks in something else.

Think about it. Is this the pathetic goal we want to set for our students? Set a low goal, and many students without any additional incentives will be satisfied with achieving D's while sitting—and sometimes sleeping—through remedial classes for the "dumb-dumbs." The tragedy is that most of the students in those classes are not dumb. And they could achieve more, learning things useful for after high school—for employment, maybe for college and for life—if challenged by higher requirements in order to participate in activities they enjoy.

After much prodding and appearances before the South Bend Community School Board, I convinced the board to follow the example of California. When Los Angeles County implemented a 2.0 grade point average (a C average) in the mid-1980s for athletes to be eligible, thousands initially were ruled ineligible. The next year, 90 percent of those met the challenge and became better students and were eligible.

Today, the state of California mandates a 2.0 minimum. And, I am proud to say, so do the high schools in the South Bend system. It was implemented in 2009.

But late in 2012, some South Bend coaches began an effort to change the requirements. *South Bend Tribune* sports columnist Al Lesar wrote about their complaining.

The playing field isn't level, they argued, because

teams from other school districts with which they compete have lower standards for participation. The other schools still can suit up kids with the five D's and an F, kids who may be very good athletes even if not bothering much with school subjects, and a South Bend school has to bench a key player who falls short of the higher standards.

I was furious.

And Lesar wrote another column, giving me a chance to respond.

"Push the right buttons and Digger Phelps' passion still bubbles," Lesar wrote. "The former Notre Dame basketball coach has taken his education advocacy from the program he mentored for 20 years to a much bigger stage, the streets of South Bend."

The critics of a C average had some cutesy arguments about street gangs not requiring a 2.0 GPA and suggesting that a kid turned away from high school sports by the requirement for decent grades will instead find welcome in a gang unconcerned about grades.

This is total nonsense. The best way to keep kids from dropping out and dropping into a gang is to give them incentives, get them interested in academics, encourage them to graduate and provide them with the fundamentals necessary for gainful employment or admission to college after that graduation.

The complaining coaches wailed over a situation in which a South Bend athlete has five C's and a C-minus and thus is not eligible. Too bad. But why didn't the coach and school administrators in such a case provide the mentoring and study opportunities for that kid to bring the C-minus up to a C or to bring one of the other grades up beyond just a C?

Now, let me make clear that I don't dislike or belittle high school coaches. Most high school coaches do a great job for little compensation, not much appreciation and often grief when fielding losing teams.

Heck. I was a junior high school basketball coach and then a high school coach and I know something about losing. I started my head coaching career in Trenton, New Jersey, at Junior High School No. 4, where they lost every game the prior year. We lost the first four. Then we started winning, at least enough that I got a job as head coach at St. Gabriel's High School in Hazelton, Pennsylvania.

So, I remember coaching at that level, an important level. And I appreciate the high school coaches that helped to develop athletes who played for me at Notre Dame. They often put in a good word for the Irish and their coach during recruitment.

But any coach arguing that academic standards should be lowered to "level the playing field" is just plain wrong about that. Lowered standards are not good for the kids. Not good for education. And high schools should be concerned first about education. Coaches, while understandably wanting to win, also should be concerned about education—concerned first abut education.

Would coaches want their own sons or daughters to slip by just barely, lessening chances of getting into a college of their choice or any college at all? Lessening also chances of even getting a job in these times when hiring requirements have become more stringent? No. And they shouldn't want that for other kids.

It's the poor kids who are exploited most by lowered standards. Some of them don't have parents in their lives who care about or encourage academics. Educators must encourage them and challenge them, not just let them drift along, satisfied with D's.

Giving a girl or boy lowered standards—almost no standards at all—because of concern about temporary loss of eligibility for sports, band, cheerleading or a position on the high school yearbook or newspaper is deplorable and harmful.

I'm familiar with tough academic requirements for athletes at Notre Dame. And the athletes rise to the challenge and go on to graduate.

As the *Chronicle of Higher Education* reported, the Notre Dame football program in 2012 became the first to earn a No. 1 ranking in the Bowl Championship Series standings while having the nation's top graduation rate as well.

One of the outstanding examples of an athlete determined to meet academic challenges is LaPhonso Ellis, a player I recruited in the Projects of East St. Louis, Illinois. When he was a junior, his high school team won a state championship—and other colleges became interested in him. His team repeated as state champions in his senior year, with Fonz the star. By then, every major program was interested.

Initially, of course, I feared that this kid, from a neighborhood where poverty prevailed, would not want a Notre Dame academic challenge—or that he couldn't meet the challenge if he did come.

But I learned more. And I was impressed. His mother insisted on her son doing homework, making grades—good grades—and not succumbing to the temptation of slipping by with C's and D's and an occasional F. She wouldn't let him just barely stay eligible. He had to take his education as seriously as his basketball.

On Nov. 17, 1987, the last day for letters of intent for the early signing period, LaPhonso would decide where he would go to college. On a table at his home for the announcement were letters of intent for the three finalists: UCLA, the University of Illinois and Notre Dame. I didn't know what he would do. In South Bend, I awaited the announcement. After the drama of the preliminaries, this big kid with such big promise picked up and signed the Notre Dame letter of intent.

Not only did he select the academic challenge of Notre Dame, he wanted a degree in accounting from the highly acclaimed Business School. Twice in his Notre Dame career he was ineligible for multiple games because of academics. While he didn't meet the Notre Dame standards, at most colleges he would have remained eligible to play. At some colleges, unfortunately, he would have been kept away from challenging courses in accounting. Tough degrees at some places are discouraged. In fact, too often there is no intent of fulfilling any degree requirements—no intent by the college, the coach or the athlete that a degree will be obtained.

My intent was for all of my players to get their degrees. All of them did. For 20 years. Two of my best players, Adrian Dantley and Gary Brokaw, both on my "first team" of players I coached at Notre Dame, left for the pros before their senior years. Both promised me they would return to get their degrees. Both did. They knew that even with big money as a pro, a Notre Dame degree is worth a lot. It's priceless.

Even at Notre Dame, LaPhonso could have switched to a less challenging degree. We aren't sadists insisting on only the toughest majors. But LaPhonso wanted that accounting degree. And he got it.

Although I left my position as Notre Dame head basketball coach before his senior year, I was back for Commencement, returning on Air Force One with President George H.W. Bush, the Commencement speaker, for whom I then was a presidential assistant running Operation Weed and Seed.

At the graduation ceremony, Fonz and Elmer Bennett, another of my players, waved their diplomas proudly for me to see. I was proud of Ellis, who got that degree before turning pro and playing for 11 years in the National Basketball Association. I was proud also of Bennett. I thought of how he hit a three-point shot at the buzzer to beat third-ranked Syracuse in a pressure-packed game before more than 32,000 fans at Syracuse.

Yes, I was proud of their basketball achievements. Right then, they were proud—so proud of getting their degrees. And for that achievement, I was so proud of them also.

Ellis has gone on after his pro career to use that accounting degree as an entrepreneur. He is the owner now of two Jamba Juice franchises and is looking to expand. He also is a basketball analyst for ESPN and for Notre Dame games.

If nobody had challenged him to get more than just some D's to slip by to eligibility in high school, he could not have made it at Notre Dame. If he hadn't challenged himself by picking Notre Dame and getting that accounting degree, would Fonz be the outstanding person, the success, he is today?

Challenges aren't bad for athletes. They are essential.

CHAPTER FOUR

NRA's Way
"Gin Up Fears"

VIOLENCE IN THE STREETS doesn't just stay there. It barges into Columbine High School, onto college campuses at Virginia Tech and Northern Illinois, into a movie theater in Colorado, into malls, offices, congressional town hall meetings and even into first-grade classrooms in Newtown, Connecticut.

My efforts are focused on curbing the shootings in the streets, where gang and drug violence so often involves young people who have dropped out of school. But we cannot ignore the horrible violence of those who drop into a school—to kill.

Guns are the common denominator. On the streets, handguns are the weapons of choice as youthful gang members use them to intimidate and sometimes to kill. They kill each other, kill innocent bystanders and even kill folks in their nearby homes as bullets fly in dangerous neighborhoods. Something many times more powerful, a military-style assault weapon, with rapid fire from 30-round magazines, was used by the killer at Sandy Hook Elementary School in Newtown to slay 20 first-graders and six adults.

We need to do something about guns. But what?

"Gun control" is the wrong term. It scares gun owners who would favor common-sense approaches but fear "control" would somehow mean taking away guns for hunting or legitimate collecting or personal safety in their homes. I don't want government "controlling" those folks. They can and should keep their guns. And they will. The Supreme Court already has ruled on that. Gun confiscation would have no chance in Congress anyway. And it's not proposed by President Obama, Vice President Biden or anybody else in the administration.

What is needed is support for common-sense restrictions on the easy access to assault weapons— weapons designed to kill on the battlefield. We also need thorough background checks for every gun purchaser. Most Americans have assumed mistakenly that we long have had rigid and universal background checks. Hardly. The gun profiteers made sure of loopholes big enough to let any maniac slip through.

Let me make this clear: I am NOT advocating the repeal of the Second Amendment right to bear arms. But let's understand that the Second Amendment doesn't prohibit common sense—or common-sense restrictions.

The Supreme Court, though upholding the right to bear arms, said that the Second Amendment is not absolute. No constitutional right is absolute. Sure, the First Amendment protects free speech. It doesn't, however, allow somebody to shout "fire" in a crowded theater. With the Second Amendment, there is no right to fire a bazooka from the rooftop.

While I long have respected the National Rifle Association, once honored for a proud history of promoting gun safety as well as defending Second Amendment rights, I deplore the present NRA leadership. They play politics to portray common sense on guns as confiscation. And they are shilling for the "blood money" profiteers selling the most deadly of weapons to the widest market of purchasers, law-abiding or not.

They put out a shooting game for kids right after the killer of the first-graders was described as addicted to shooting videos. They targeted the president's kids in a "sick" commercial.

The "real" NRA members, the people I respect and want to protect from any "control" that restricts legitimate rights, must be going nuts to hear they're now represented by...well...nuts.

With his commentaries, Joe Scarborough, host of "Morning Joe" on MSNBC, was the first to convince me that the NRA left us. We were not turning away from the NRA that we had known. Joe has been kind in letting me appear many times on his highly rated program to talk of many causes from New Orleans recovery to prostate cancer prevention, from successful Memphis charter school innovations to my efforts to coach the streets in South Bend and elsewhere.

Scarborough is a conservative, advocating small government, low taxes and a balanced budget. He is a former Republican congressman from Florida and a longtime defender of Second Amendment rights for hunting and protection in the home. He is the proud possessor of the top rating from the NRA for his votes in Congress.

After Newtown and the unfeeling, unacceptable and unreasonable response of the NRA, Joe couldn't take it any longer. Neither can I.

Here is what Scarborough said as he broke with a broken NRA leadership:

> This is not, for the NRA, about Second Amendment rights. Justice Scalia clearly laid out in Heller what Second Amendment rights were and what they were not. The most conservative justice on the Supreme Court, Antonin Scalia, made it very clear assault weapons were not protected by the Second Amendment. This is not about protecting the Second Amendment.

What is it about?

Money.

Not just money that comes to the NRA as it uses scare tactics to bring in new memberships. There's much more.

Joe Scarborough explained it succinctly this way:

> This is about gun manufacturers making millions and millions and millions of dollars. This is about retailers making millions and millions and millions of dollars.
>
> Do you know how much money these people have made over the slaughter of 20 innocents in Newtown? Do you know how much richer these rich gun manufacturers have gotten over the past month, and how the NRA uses that tragedy to gin up fears, and websites use that tragedy to gin up fears that they're coming to take your guns away?
>
> Hey, got a message for you: They can't take your guns away. We've got something called the Second Amendment in the Constitution of the United States. Justice Scalia said in 2009 they can't come and take our guns away. You can have a handgun to protect your family. But outside of that, they can regulate guns.

I agree with Joe, as do most gun owners and NRA members, when he said that the assault rifle that blasted away 20 little first-graders "changed everything."

Politicians, even if coveting a top-ranked NRA rating for their next campaign, need to show the courage to protect children as well as protect legitimate Second Amendment rights.

Show courage?

Forty-five members of the U.S. Senate did not.

They voted "no" on realistic background checks for gun purchases, preventing passage of a common-sense measure to make the nation safer—a common-sense measure overwhelmingly supported by the public.

This had nothing to do with taking away any-body's guns. Nothing to do with taking away rights of law-abiding citizens to purchase guns—nothing to do with the Second Amendment. Everything to do, however, with closing loopholes that allow peo-ple who are not law-abiding at all—criminals, gang members, terrorists—and people with severe mental problems to easily obtain guns.

On the morning after what President Obama rightfully called a "shameful" vote by the 45, Joe Scarborough ripped into the cowardice. On his TV program, he displayed the photos, one by one, of the "cowards," 41 Republicans and four Democrats.

Joe, the former Republican congressman and out-spoken advocate of conservative fiscal policy, was par-ticularly harsh on his fellow Republicans in the Senate, many of whom he has had as guests on his program. "You do not ignore 90 percent of the American people on an issue of public safety," he said, citing polls show-ing extensive support for background checks.

"Mark it down, this is going to be a turning point in the history of the Republican Party," Joe said. He added:

> This party that killed this background check yesterday—this party is moving toward ex-tinction. A new Republican Party is going

to replace it. And this is going to be a vote that people are going to look back on and say, "That party—that extremism—that was unsustainable."

I am a Democrat. But as I have often said, I was a Reagan Democrat, willing to support Republicans when I felt that some Democratic candidates and leaders had left me, had strayed too far to the left. I served in a Republican administration, an appointee of President George H.W. Bush. I'm not a highly partisan guy. I take no pleasure in seeing either party drift too far toward one extreme or the other.

Preventing violence in this country should not be a Democratic thing or a Republican thing. It should be an American thing, with our senators thinking of what's right for the nation, not cowering before any lobby or playing politics with this issue. Politicians shouldn't play with guns.

Guns are not evil. But they're too often used for evil in this country. That's why studies show that the overall risk of being murdered is higher in America than it is in any other first-world democracy.

Guns don't kill people. True, not by themselves. People using guns kill people. And they can kill a whole lot more people with an assault rifle. Fewer people would have opportunities to kill if real background checks—checks before all gun purchases—kept guns out of the hands of people with serious criminal or mental problems.

Sure, some people denied access to a gun could still find ways to kill. The angry wielder of a potato masher could mash a victim fatally. But he is not likely with his potato masher to smash into a school and kill 20 little kids and six adults.

While guns are not in themselves evil, they also are not something to be worshiped or glorified. The rapid-fire Bushmaster assault weapon with quick-loading 30-round magazines used to shoot the little kids at Sandy Hook Elementary School again and again and again was not evil. The killer who fired it again and again and again was evil.

Was the availability of that firepower an evil? Yes. A preventable evil.

And, in any event, should this weapon be glorified? Should Bushmaster enthusiasts brag about the deadly weapon? Especially now?

The Bushmaster website (well after Sandy Hook) in 2013 still offered some merchandise aimed at promoting—or, you could say, glorifying—the weapon of choice in the school slaughter. For instance, you could order a Bushmaster bomber fur cap, with the snake and rifle logo, for just $26. Or you could get a t-shirt promoting the Bushmaster, sizes from small to double extra-large, for only $19.99.

Bushmaster logos also were featured on caps for $12. Now that would be a nice cap to wear in Newtown.

For $47, you could get a large Bushmaster rifle

case, "perfect for storing an ACR (adoptive combat rifle) with mounted optics, spare magazines, alternate stocks, hand guards, barrels—just about anything that you're accessorizing your ACR with." But wait. There's more. Would you like a "discreet carrying case," hiding the fact that you are headed somewhere for some reason with such firepower?

These Bushmaster website items are not illegal. No suggestion that they are. But is the glorification of this weapon what we need right after Sandy Hook? I think we need something else—common-sense restrictions on assault rifles designed for the battlefield—specifically, common-sense restrictions to keep them on the battlefield and out of our schools.

CHAPTER FIVE

Music City
"You HAVE Overcome."

There's a town that I call home
Where all the streets are paved with soul.
Down on Beale, there's a honky-tonk bar,
Hear the wail of a blues guitar,
Have a beer and drop a dime in a blind man's jar.

The blues sing softly in the air,
Like a Sunday morning prayer–
Just one more drink and you'll see God everywhere.
Like a sad old melody–
That tears you up but sets you free–
That's how Memphis lives in me.

There comes a time when muddy waters run rough.
There comes a point when a man has had enough.
Like a friend who always stands by me,
Memphis knows me,
Memphis shows me
How this life just has to be.

I couldn't even try to run away, say goodbye.
Here I was born, and here is where I'll die.
Just a man from Tennessee,
Can't be what I can't be–
All I know is Memphis lives in me.

Just a man from Tennessee
Can't be what I can't be–
All I know is Memphis lives,
All I know is Memphis gives,
All I know is Memphis lives in me!

Those are the lyrics of "Memphis Lives in Me" from the popular musical *Memphis*. The show is based, with poetic license, on the career of Memphis disc jockey Dewey Phillips, a white DJ who, in the 1950s, dared to play and popularize traditional black music. He is said to be the first to play Elvis Presley records on Memphis radio.

Memphis sound had its influence not only on Elvis but also on the styles of Jerry Lee Lewis, Johnny Cash, Roy Orbison, B.B. King and scores of other performers. It has a central role in the history of music in America—rock-n-roll, rockabilly, blues, gospel and jazz.

Performers, both the established and the newcomers hoping to launch successful careers, still draw crowds to the famous Beale Street spots. Graceland stands as a monument to Elvis.

Memphis is indeed "Music City."

Because of that, it made sense that a new charter school opening in Memphis in 2005 would have an emphasis on music and would appeal to students with an interest in the musical heritage of their city and the opportunities there or elsewhere in music. Just as a culinary high school made sense in New Orleans, with its famed cuisine and opportunities in the restaurant field, this school with its concentration on music made sense in Memphis.

Thus was born the Soulsville Stax Music Academy Charter School. I heard about it as it developed a reputation for excellence in academics and as a way to get kids off the streets in the surrounding inner-city neighborhood. I visited. And I was so impressed that I have become involved in fundraising for the school and have sought in many television interviews to put in plugs for the school and this concept that could be successful in other cities as well.

I was honored to be one of the commencement speakers in 2012 for the first high school graduation there. This school started with just one grade—sixth—and only 60 students when it opened and it expanded each year, in enrollment and in years of study, to 480 students in grades six through twelve.

Impressive test scores are achieved, but most impressive of all is that all 51 graduating seniors at that first commencement were accepted for college, with scholarships totaling more than $3.2 million.

How do they do it? The mission statement tells the story succinctly: "The Soulsville Charter School will prepare students for success in college and in life in an academically rigorous, music-rich environment." The school describes itself as offering really "a revolution, a force rising up against ordinary expectations and the status quo of public education in Memphis."

Yes, there is music, but there also is emphasis on core academic courses and preparation for college. A third of the students are from the Soulsville inner-city neighborhood.

One of the first graduates, just turning 18, had tears in his eyes as he thought of his outlook back when he started as a sixth-grader in that first class. With the gangs and the violence in the streets of his neighborhood, he thought he would be dead by 18. Now he was heading for college instead of the morgue.

The kids in that school simply don't have time to wander dangerous streets. And they don't want to. They become hooked on education and opportunity, not what is peddled on those streets.

Soulsville Charter School has a lengthy school day, starting at 7:45 a.m. each day and continuing until 4:30 p.m. Monday through Thursday and until 2:15 p.m. on Friday. There are at least four Saturday sessions. An extended school year begins in August and runs until the end of June. In addition, there is a required three-week summer session primarily spent on the Rhodes College campus to give students an early exposure to college.

As the kids move through the grades, learning responsibility and respect and developing a sense of pride in their school, they help to run the place, guiding the new sixth-graders on expectations.

"We don't do that here," they tell a newcomer who gets out of line. "We do it this way. Here are the rules."

On the morning of that Soulsville commencement ceremony, as I was thinking of what I would tell the graduates, I visited again the site where Dr. Martin Luther King Jr. was shot, the old Lorraine Motel on Mulberry Street. It's part of a museum now, but you still can look up to the balcony on the second floor and see the wreath marking where King stood outside his room when he was slain on April 4, 1968.

I told the graduates and their proud parents and other relatives about going there and thinking again about how this great leader used the words of the civil rights song to proclaim that "We Shall Overcome." And I said that surely Dr. King was looking down from heaven, "looking down at you, with a smile on his face, saying, 'You HAVE Overcome.'"

Indeed, they had.

If New Orleans can build a culinary high school geared to needs and interests there, and thereby help kids to overcome, and if Memphis, "Music City," can develop a successful music-rich charter school to help kids there to overcome, why can't other cities come up with innovative ideas like that for their kids? They can. Some have. Most haven't. But all should. It's not that costly to find ways to keep kids in school, off the streets—to overcome.

Certainly the cost of helping them to become productive citizens is not as costly to society as the alternative.

CHAPTER SIX

After Katrina
"Walking to New Orleans"

I LISTENED TO THE WORDS. And I cried. It's a sorry person, man or woman, even if normally viewed as tough and strong, that never cares enough to have tears come to their eyes.

Tears come to most of us possessing human feelings at such times as the death of a parent or some terrible accident or illness striking a spouse, a child, a close friend. But the plight of people you don't even know also can have most of us choked up, with tears welling. The shooting of the first-graders in Newtown, Connecticut, was such an event.

The words that brought tears to my eyes were in the lyrics of a song recorded in 1960, back when I was a freshman at Rider College in Trenton, New Jersey, planning then to become an undertaker and join in the operation of my father's funeral home in Beacon, New York.

When I heard the tune as a pop hit and then myriad times over the decades as it became a traditional song about a city I often visited—a favorite city—it certainly brought no feelings of sadness then.

Well, I watched television coverage of the devastation of that city, New Orleans, when Hurricane Katrina struck on Aug. 29, 2005. For days we saw the sadness, the tragedy—people clustered on roofs, trapped by the waters; people pleading for rescue at the Superdome. Then I saw a picture of the man who sang that song being carried out of his home by rescuers. And I went out to buy a CD with the song that was made a hit by legendary New Orleans pianist and singer-songwriter Fats Domino. He initially was reported to have died when waters flooded the Lower 9th Ward, where he lived.

The song is titled "Walking to New Orleans."

The lyrics:

> This time I'm walkin' to New Orleans
> I'm walkin' to New Orleans
> I'm gonna need two pair of shoes
> When I get through walkin' these blues
> When I get back to New Orleans
>
> I've got my suitcase in my hand
> Now ain't that a shame?
> I'm leavin' here today
> Yes, I'm goin' back home to stay
> Yes, I'm walkin' to New Orleans

You used to be my honey
'Til you spent all my money
No use for you to cry
I'll see you by and by
'Cause I'm walkin' to New Orleans

I've got no time for talkin'
I've got to keep on walkin'
New Orleans is my home
That's the reason why I'm goin'
Yes, I'm walkin' to New Orleans

I'm walkin' to New Orleans
I'm walkin' to New Orleans

I knew then that, even if I wouldn't be walkin' to get there, I'd be going to New Orleans to try to do something to help. After we learned about what a terrible job FEMA was doing to help and how suffering was continuing, I knew that I would do more than just go to visit and offer help to two of my former Notre Dame basketball players from New Orleans.

Through recruiting players there, I got to know New Orleans well and to love its history, spirit and great cuisine. Longtime Irish basketball fans will remember well my two players from New Orleans, Donald Royal, a 6-8 forward on our 1983-87 teams, and Tim Singleton, a 6-1 point guard on the 1987-91 teams.

Recruiting isn't always fun. There are several reasons for that: travel to out-of-the-way destinations; at times, the difficulty convincing skeptical high school

47

stars and their parents that Notre Dame isn't in a bidding war and offers no "signing bonus" or exception from academic standards; and, after extensive recruiting, you can lose a player, perhaps due to false rumors planted by another college. Definitely not always fun.

But recruiting Donald Royal was fun. Not only was there the happy ending of bringing one of my best and one of my favorite players to Notre Dame, there was also the opportunity while visiting Donald's high school, St. Augustine, to see its outstanding band—a band that has performed at New Orleans Saints games and rivals the rhythm of the famed bands at Grambling. And then there's the cuisine—like having lunch at Dooky Chase's, my favorite restaurant in a city of great restaurants.

For years after my first visit to Dooky Chase's, I would return for the wonderful food, to view the African-American art in a place where so many in the civil rights movement in the 1960s (including Dr. Martin Luther King, Jr.) met and planned, and to talk with Leah Chase, known as the queen of Creole cuisine. Leah would always send back with me some frozen gumbo to be thawed at home so I could enjoy a taste of New Orleans in South Bend.

Katrina flooded Dooky's. Members of the Chase family were existing in a FEMA trailer rather than preparing red beans and rice. Now, they are back.

In basketball, as in other endeavors, a great first

step means a lot. Royal had a great first step and his ability to drive into the lane so fast led to his being fouled a lot. Donald could draw fouls and hit free throws. An example is a game against Syracuse in the always-tough-on-visitors Carrier Dome, when he had three baskets but also was 14 of 17 from the free-throw line in a win that propelled us to one of the 14 NCAA Tournament bids we received. Donald went on to make a living at the free-throw line in the National Basketball Association, where he played for eight seasons.

Tim Singleton brought me back to New Orleans to recruit a fine student and unselfish player who was captain of my last Notre Dame team. Tim played in 112 games at Notre Dame, 70 of them as my starting point guard. But he never hit a three-point shot. No problem. Shooting was not his job. He brought the ball down the court against any defensive pressure and distributed it to players in position to shoot. He had the respect of the team, vital for a point guard.

When I finally was able to get in touch with them, I found that Singleton had lost almost everything in Katrina, while Royal escaped severe damage.

"Brownie, you're doing a heck of a job," so claimed President George W. Bush, hailing the bureaucrat heading the FEMA effort.

No, it wasn't a good job. Help was slow in coming, or coming not at all, and often was misdirected, with Washington bureaucrats thinking that belatedly plopping down all those unsightly and unhealthy FEMA trailers was a solution.

Nearly two years after Katrina, in the Lower 9th Ward, a poorer area of the city that had been hit by a wall of water as high as rooftops, a barge that the storm had flung into homes with deadly destruction still remained there as a horrible reminder, a horrible sight.

Street after street, for blocks, for miles, it still looked like the pictures of bombed-out German cities at the close of World War II. The French Quarter, on higher ground, was getting back. But businesses in the hardest hit areas were not.

Fats Domino was seeking restoration of his devastated home, where symbols of his honors of a lifetime had been swept away. Many former residents who had fled the city were never to return.

"For rent" signs were displayed in windows of structures that had become mostly piles of debris. What's to rent? "For sale" signs were scrawled on windows of other crumbled structures. Buy what? Buy where? "For lease" signs were propped up at doorways that once had doors. A long-term lease? For how long could that thing remain standing?

But I wasn't waiting. I went to the South Bend Rotary Club, the club that helped with my efforts to fix up deteriorating schools in the city, and asked for help as a sponsoring organization for a new project—my project to build new homes in New Orleans. I donated

$90,000 for the first home, not so I could brag about it, but because you should put your money where your mouth is if you're asking others to contribute.

Rotary clubs and members were soon to add $45,000. Others joined in as well, and we were underway, ready to build a first house and select a worthy family in desperate need of decent housing.

The name of my project: "Walking to New Orleans."

I couldn't pick the right family, but I knew who could. I contacted Rev. Joseph Doyle, president of St. Augustine High School, in a devastated area where families were in desperate need of decent housing. Father Doyle had tough requirements in finding a successful applicant, including work history to indicate the family could make payments on a $30,000 mortgage and maintain the home. Involvement in community activities also was important.

Walter and Shirley Collins and their three children were selected. Among the reasons were their own heroic efforts to save people from the raging floodwaters of Katrina. They moved into their new home, completely furnished, just before Christmas in 2007.

It was emotional, for them—and for me, to see their delight. Television coverage kind of startled them, but it was needed for a central purpose—to encourage others elsewhere to do things on their own to help New Orleans.

Walter and Shirley helped about 20 people to find refuge in the high point of their two-story house when the waters raged higher and higher. They saw people die, even thought they might die, and were separated in the rescue effort. Neither knew whether the other had survived until Walter was able to get his cell phone recharged. He called Shirley's number, hoping that she was alive.

She answered. She was in Houston. So was he. The family soon was reunited and went back to New Orleans.

So, after the success with the first family—a family soon to add on to their house and provide landscaping to enhance the value—we set out to build a second home. I wanted two, in recognition of my two recruits from New Orleans.

Then, in October of 2009, I was able to provide another home for another family, Alrich and Inell Elders and their two children. Again I contributed. But so did so many others, like the shoppers at South Bend area Martin's Super Markets who tossed in dimes, quarters and dollars, raising $5,000 that paid for furniture. The faculty at Notre Dame's Mendoza College of Business raised $22,000.

The new home for the Elders is in an area where houses had literally been washed away by Katrina. The neighborhood was coming back.

"I cried and my heart was filled with joy," said Inell in an interview about her reaction to getting the keys to their new home. Bringing joy to her and her family, and bringing another home where there had been devastation, also brought joy to those of us with our own version of "Walking to New Orleans."

CHAPTER SEVEN

Culinary School
"Was a Sorry Mess"

NEW ORLEANS needs more than new houses.

Jobs are needed, especially jobs that pay a living wage. Unemployment and underemployment woes are not unique to New Orleans, of course, but they were exacerbated there by the winds and waters of Katrina. Many stores, offices and other places of employment were ruined—many gone for good.

Even before Katrina, unemployment was high. There were inner-city neighborhoods with widespread poverty and resulting problems with gangs, drugs and violence.

Tourists coming to see New Orleans didn't see those neighborhoods. They came for the city's history, entertainment, fine spring and fall weather and unique cuisine, not to witness gang violence. Conventioneers didn't see those neighborhoods. They wandered through the French Quarter, not through the areas of poverty. Fans streaming into the Super-dome for a New Orleans Saints game didn't see those neighborhoods. They were interested in highly-paid athletes who have made it to the NFL, not young men of the same age who have no job and no hope really of ever making it anywhere.

Back when I was directing Operation Weed and Seed for President George H.W. Bush, I saw those neighborhoods. These were areas that did not share in the prosperity brought to the more affluent by the throngs coming for Mardi Gras, for vacations, for conventions, for sporting events. People from those areas couldn't afford to go to the fine restaurants and never walked into the convention hotels, unless it was to clean the rooms.

With the concentrated force of federal agencies and local assistance, at Operation Weed and Seed we would seek to weed out the crime and drugs in trou-bled city neighborhoods. Then we would seed posi-tive programs to keep these areas from regressing. In New Orleans there was a real challenge to find a way to sow the seeds of economic empowerment. We had limited funds. So we searched for ways to use com-munity assets already in place for the seeding phase of providing alternatives to crime and violence. We needed to enhance opportunities for employment, especially for young people.

The U.S. attorney in New Orleans came up with a suggestion I quickly embraced. The idea was to take advantage of a great community asset: the unique cuisine—the great Cajun and Creole food and other specialties—from the po' boy sandwiches at unpretentious little eateries to the Oysters Rockefeller created at the swanky Antoine's.

There were job openings in the restaurants and in catering. There were also opportunities to start new places to attract even more visitors to experience the dining highlights of the city. But many of the unemployed lacked the skills to fill the openings, often lacking even the knowledge of where the openings were or how to gain the skills to apply successfully.

We knew that many unemployed single moms in public housing were no doubt good cooks, able to whip up inexpensive but darn good red beans and rice and gumbo. We lined up chefs and restaurant owners for some mentoring. They provided training and advice in how to prepare food in larger quantities so that these women could fill openings in restaurants and in catering at conventions, parties, receptions and other events where New Orleans-style food is served.

This is a concept I have carried even further in responding to Katrina. We now have success in transforming a battered high school, in a hard-hit area, into a new culinary high school that will give kids a chance to find employment where employees are needed in their city and even potentially to go on to become restaurant owners or great chefs themselves.

John McDonogh High School is the place. It was built in 1902 and needed a whole lot of refurbishing before Katrina. After the flooding from the hurricane, it was a sorry mess.

I went there for a live appearance on Nov. 20, 2009, on "Morning Joe," the MSNBC program hosted by Joe Scarborough and Mika Brzezinski. They have done a wonderful job of focusing on the plight of New Orleans after most of the nation has forgotten the devastation there and the long, continuing struggle to recover. I stood on the basketball court, with the surface bulging in waves from the flooding, and issued a challenge for somebody to do something about it. Actually, I picked the somebody, Robbins Sports Surfaces. I hailed that company as providing the surfaces for home courts of championship teams, from the Los Angeles Lakers in the pros to North Carolina in college.

And I said: "I'm going to challenge this company in Cincinnati, Robbins Sports Surfaces, to rebuild this floor." Some of the people there thought I was crazy.

Within two hours there was a man there with a clipboard measuring the court size for installation of that new floor. The man was Joe Covington, Jr., of the Birmingham based Covington Flooring Co., the regional distributor-installer for Robbins.

Covington told the *Times-Picayune* newspaper in New Orleans that he was in the city that day for a business trip. He said he began getting e-mail messages and cell phone calls from people in his company and Robbins. They had viewed the challenge on "Morning Joe."

"I got dressed hurriedly," Covington said, and quickly conferred with Robbins officials and headed out to measure the floor.

"Morning Joe" was off the air when he got there, but MSNBC broke in with the live update of the quick response to the challenge.

The floor has been installed. Kids on the basketball team or just participating in intramurals now can dribble a basketball and have it bounce back into their hands rather than bouncing wildly away from them off an undulating floor surface.

On a later program, during which I joined in an exciting announcement at John McDonogh about its future as a culinary school, Joe Scarborough noted the new floor and said of my challenge: "He shook 'em down."

Well, I suppose I put them on the spot. But I'd like to look at it as the type of challenge to which corporate America is willing to listen and to which it will respond. Corporate officials have a stake in America, too, and many of them are eager to help—so long as they know that their contributions won't be wasted and will make a positive difference.

That visit to the high school at which I issued the challenge also brought in other substantial contributions in response to the pleas from Joe and Mika to remember New Orleans. There was a $125,000 contribution from Starbucks. A publishing company donated textbooks. There were donations for a college tour for the seniors. Small donations were welcome, too.

The newspaper reported that it all added up to over $200,000 on that day, not even counting the future new gym floor. The funds were put to good use, including getting a new roof so no kid would need to sit under an umbrella at a school assembly.

The best news of all came in another "Morning Joe" announcement on March 28, 2012, at John McDonogh High School. Louisiana Superintendent of Education John White was there with me to announce that the state would provide $35 million for a complete makeover of the school "to make this the best culinary and college preparation school in this state."

The superintendent, who had run New Orleans schools for a Recovery School District after the hurricane, shared my enthusiasm for training kids in the culinary arts, skills needed for jobs now and for the opportunity to someday be great chefs or restaurant owners.

While the school will offer that specialty, it also will stress the basics of education and preparation for college.

Will this help kids who might otherwise be lost on the streets? Yes. How many? I don't know. But if it's only a few—and I think it will be many more—it will change some lives and save other lives in lessening street violence.

Columnist's Opinion
"Speaks from the Heart"

IT'S KIND OF AWKWARD to try to describe your own passion for a cause.

But David Haugh, the premier sports columnist for the *Chicago Tribune*, captured my cause and my feelings, my passion, in his Sept. 2, 2012, column. David was very kind in telling of my efforts and very accurate in his description of the projects I support from South Bend to Memphis to New Orleans. Perhaps he caught attention in Chicago for the need of similar efforts against violence there. David granted permission to reprint his column here:

> SOUTH BEND, Ind.—Desperation brought Digger Phelps to the Adams High School auditorium one night last April. Inspiration made him rise.
>
> Phelps, the colorful former Notre Dame basketball coach and current ESPN analyst,

had returned from the Final Four to his home of the last 40 years when a *South Bend Tribune* headline ruined his first night off in weeks: "City sees youth violence spike."

For years Phelps had led local mentoring programs intended to stop the violence. But now, he wondered, for what? Over the first 10 days of April, five South Bend teens had been shot in three separate incidents. In the coaching vernacular Phelps assigns to everyday life, he was losing big. His city was losing control. And this was no game.

So when new South Bend Community Schools Superintendent Carole Schmidt called a Town Hall meeting to address concerns in the district, Phelps meticulously went over his personal game plan. As usual, it relied heavily on instinct and adrenalin.

"There are about 200 people there and I get up and ask, 'OK, how can we put a team together of community assets to resolve this issue of youth violence, with education being the foundation?'" Phelps recalled. "She says, 'The community has to come together.'"

Phelps, 71 going on 40, suddenly felt a familiar pang coaches who live for challenges never lose.

"I jump and say, 'I'll coach it!'" Phelps said. "I had no idea I was going to do that. Not sure what made me."

Richard Phelps was 12 when his father, Dick, an undertaker in the town of Beacon, N.Y., made clear to him and his sisters how to treat grieving families at their new funeral home.

"He says, 'You kids understand: All religions are our religions. All skin colors are our skin colors. All cultures are our cultures. When people lose a loved one, they trust us through that crisis. Treat people in need right,'" Phelps said. "That never left me."

Phelps' dad, an active community leader, grew up in an orphanage and never knew his father. An uncle adopted Dick Phelps as a teenager and gave him a future. When Digger tells young kids from single-parent homes they can overcome their circumstances to make an impact on society, he thinks of his father. When Phelps wonders if a kid is worth the effort, he remembers he wouldn't have the life he enjoys if somebody with good intentions had left his dad alone.

"I see kids who just need someone to say, 'You don't have to go this way, just trust, there's someone who cares,'" Phelps said.

————

There are 54 names and phone numbers on the spreadsheet. For two months beginning in mid-April, Phelps worked eight hours a day contacting everybody he knew in South Bend—and everybody knows Digger. He only expects the people he calls "community assets" to follow three simple rules familiar to Phelps' former players: Don't assume. Follow up. Have a backup.

"Hi, this is Digger Phelps of Notre Dame,"

Phelps said over the phone when the St. Joseph County prosecutor's office answered.

Phelps coached his last game at Notre Dame in 1991, but adults in town still associate him with the place he went 393-195 over 20 seasons but is remembered best for graduating all 56 players who played four years for him. As for younger fans, Phelps kidded, "They know me as the guy on ESPN who matches his ties with his highlighters."

One of those kids needs Phelps' brand of tough love now. A potential Division I basketball player, the 14-year-old got kicked out of school after being caught with drugs and a gun. Where some people might see a statistic, Phelps sees a good kid who made a bad decision. He recently accompanied the youth's probation officer for a visit at the juvenile-justice center.

"It was vintage locker room," Phelps said. "I ripped him. 'You know that basketball is worth a $200,000 education? Get with the program!' Sometimes it takes letting them know someone cares."

Ambitiously, Phelps seeks 500 new mentors so the program can start in grade school. So far he has commitments from 400. With cooperation from school and government leaders, the mentors soon will implement the kind of comprehensive after-school programs and community policing efforts he thinks can work in cities of all sizes.

"You give me a kid who is 6 for 10 years,

we've got him," Phelps said. "I don't want kids dead at 18 or 25. Grab these guys early and get them to stop killing each other."

Phelps speaks from the heart but also experience. Under President George H.W. Bush, he headed Operation Weed and Seed, an initiative intended to assist America's most struggling urban areas. In New Orleans, Phelps recently helped restore troubled McDonogh High into a culinary training center thanks to $35 million in federal funding. In Memphis, he raised funds and delivered the commencement address to the first class of students—all 51 are college-bound—at Soulsville Stax Music Academy Charter School in the city's poorest section.

"I left there thinking, why aren't we doing this all over the country?" Phelps said.

———

Like at Notre Dame, not everybody appreciates Phelps' coaching style. South Bend Councilman Henry Davis Jr. walked out of a meeting last May after accusing Phelps of grandstanding. At the same meeting, another councilman shouted at Phelps for interrupting him.

"Give me a technical," Phelps said. "I don't care about protocol if it stops kids getting shot."

He cares about progress like the Kraft executive who offered to start a youth jobs program. Like his buddy from the Bureau of Alcohol, Tobacco, Firearms and Explosives who has brought advanced gang-resistance training to

South Bend schools. Like the local clergymen Phelps challenged to "preach it on Sunday and reach them on Monday," who have increased the pool of participants.

"It will not turn things around overnight but Digger's program is a great start," South Bend Councilman Derek Dieter said. "Nobody else in this town has stepped up like him. He could be playing golf. Or with his grandkids. I love the guy. He can be abrasive but that's the coach in him saying, 'Come on, let's go.'"

———

One recent summer night, Phelps pulled up to a busy outdoor basketball court on campus. Old habits die hard.

"I said, 'Everybody up, team meeting,'" Phelps said.

Soon he was surrounded. In typical Phelps fashion, he challenged his captive audience to seek an education. To stay out of trouble. To "live the dream," Phelps said. He shared the story of Mavericks forward Bernard James, who finished his Florida State career at 27.

An athletic 24-year-old named Larry paid closer attention than the rest. Two weeks later, Phelps got word Larry had enrolled in vocational school with the goal of playing at a local junior college. He also received a text: "Hello, Mr. Phelps. Just want to keep you posted on the dream. I'm chasing."

———

Six years after Phelps quit coaching, he ran

into one of his role models—Rev. Theodore M. Hesburgh. Of all the stories about a man who influenced popes, presidents and social change, one of Phelps' favorites involves the retired Notre Dame president challenging José Napoleón Duarte.

In 1960, Duarte was a successful civil engineer when Hesburgh urged him to delve into politics in his native El Salvador. The Notre Dame alum returned home, committed himself to bringing democracy to his country and in 1984 became its president.

"So Hesburgh asks me in '97, 'What are you doing?'" Phelps said. "I had a good gig at ESPN and started a mentoring program in town. And I'll never forget it. He said, 'That's it?'"

Phelps thought of Hesburgh's expectations seeing the headline last April that changed his summer. He thinks of Hesburgh, 95, every day he tries changing a world that could be pretty comfortable if Phelps just cared about his corner.

The two shared dinner two weeks ago. "Father Hesburgh asked me what I was up to," Phelps said. "I said, 'You have me coaching the streets. I'm not Duarte but I'm getting there.'"

CHAPTER NINE

A Plan
With a "BAM"

HERE IS THE PLAN to combat neighborhood violence:

* Expand mentoring for at-risk kids;
* Involve businesses, joining with non-profit organizations and members of the community, in a team effort to provide positive alternatives;
* Build community support in neighborhoods most impacted by violence;
* Promote programs such as a basketball league to encourage competition on the court for young males who might otherwise be competing in dangerous ways on the streets;
* Seek innovative methods to keep kids in school and improve the high school graduation rate.

Here is what the mayor said about this "unprecedented coalition" to combat the shocking increase in violence that the city was experiencing:

There are proven and successful programs in our city that are creating a brighter future for some of our most vulnerable children. It is time for our city to come together and invest in them. The greatest thing we can do as a city is give our children the support they need to build a successful life, and I will work tirelessly to provide safe alternatives that reduce the risk of our kids getting involved with drugs, gangs and violence.

Sounds like my game plan for action after I was shocked by the April 10, 2012, front-page story in South Bend, my town, about the spike in youth violence. Well, it is like my plan. But the plan outlined above, and the mayoral quote about it, are from a Feb. 20, 2013, announcement by Chicago Mayor Rahm Emanuel.

Now, I'm not suggesting Chicago copied South Bend's plan. I am declaring that both cities, responding to increased violence, have found similar methods, proven methods, to combat it.

I didn't just come up with a game plan out of the blue. Never did while coaching basketball at Notre Dame. Never would do so with a plan to combat violence. To devise an effective game plan, whether in sports or in a strategy against violence, it's necessary to know the opponent, know what your team can do and know what has or hasn't worked in the past.

I've known this opponent—drugs, gangs and violence—since my days directing Operation Weed and Seed for President George H.W. Bush and then in going on with the other projects of mentoring and after-school programs and helping with troubled neighborhoods and at-risk kids in Memphis and New Orleans as well as in South Bend. I've seen what effective teamwork can do in a community. And I've found what works and what sounds good but fails to produce results.

Even though I was confident we had developed an effective game plan in South Bend, it was heartening to hear that Mayor Emanuel, with all of his advisors and resources in Chicago, had come up with a similar plan.

Chicago already had a detailed "scouting report" on strategies that work in helping at-risk kids in the game of life. A study released in 2012 by the University of Chicago Crime Lab showed the remarkable success of a Chicago program for at-risk male youth. It's called BAM (Becoming A Man) and has an after-school sports component through World Sport Chicago.

The Chicago program, right along the lines of what we are trying to do to help at-risk kids in South Bend, involves mentoring, counseling on violence avoidance, stress on the importance of education and after-school sports sessions.

Results? The University of Chicago Crime Lab study showed:

* A decrease in violent crime arrests by 44 percent;

* The reduction of failing grades by 37 percent;
* An increase in graduation rates by 10 to 23 percent.

The University of Chicago Crime Lab was established in 2008 to look scientifically, not just emotionally, at the causes and prevention of violent crime and to give policymakers solid information on what approaches really work.

This study on results is important in helping policymakers decide where to allocate limited funds, in encouraging community and business support for effective programs, and in dealing with some of the uninformed critics who spread misinformation harmful to anti-crime efforts.

Chicago's mayor is one policymaker convinced of the cost effectiveness of BAM. He cited the impressive results found in the University of Chicago study in announcing additional funding from the city in this effort to stem the rise in youth violence. And the effort won't be funded only by the city. Mayor Emanuel announced mobilization of "an unprecedented coalition" from the city's business and philanthropic communities to raise $50 million to expand the programs to help at-risk youth.

Allstate Insurance immediately pledged $5 million over five years for the communitywide effort to reduce violent crime. Wow! Five million. That's a lot. But there is a "wow" factor beyond the dollar amount. It signals a willingness of corporate America to help in this cause. Tom Wilson, Allstate chief executive officer, said in pledging the money:

> We need to all come together to take a stand and improve our neighborhoods. This is an opportunity for businesses, non-profits, foundations and individuals to make a difference and save lives. United together, we will make Chicago safer and more vibrant, so our children will prosper and build a brighter future for all of us.

That call will resonate to bring more corporate involvement—needed involvement. Wilson also agreed to spearhead the drive for $50 million along with another corporate leader, Jim Reynolds, chief executive officer of Loop Capital Investment Bank. Reynolds said this was "a strong call for all of us to come together in reducing violence in our neighborhoods, and we expect the business community to play an important and active role in answering that call."

This Chicago effort will more than triple the number of kids going through the program, from 600 to 2,000. An expanded effort is needed as shown in a Crime Lab finding that there were about 7,000 students who have missed over 40 days of school and are enrolled in schools located in a Chicago area with a homicide rate more than twice the national average.

Policymakers now have statistics showing that BAM and programs like it can be an important step— not a solution, but a step that works—as they search for answers.

Another program found to be effective in Chicago is Windy City Hoops, a year-round basketball league aimed at encouraging at-risk young adults to shoot basketballs rather than guns. Sound familiar? Exactly what I've been preaching.

Results? More than 15,000 registrations in Chicago's basketball programs, including open gym, leagues, instructional programs and camps. It's the same enthusiasm we have found in South Bend. Give kids an alternative, an opportunity, and many of them will take it. Not all. But a lot, enough that policymakers, seeing the enthusiasm and the proven results shown in the Crime Lab study, know that there is something to be done other than just build bigger prisons.

Crime Lab statistics showing the effectiveness of programs such as BAM and its sports component should encourage businesses to get behind our similar efforts in South Bend and also encourage business participation in other cities concerned with combating youth violence. Business wants to help and actually will do so when convinced of the value of these programs.

Many folks living in neighborhoods with rampant crime and gang and drug activity also will help if convinced they can make a difference. They can. They too can help with mentoring, with after-school programs, with neighborhood-watch efforts. Statistics on how all of this helps will encourage them to work to save their neighborhoods, not surrender them to gangs and crime.

The Crime Lab findings of how successful these programs can be should serve also to shut up (or at least drown out) uninformed critics who spread misinformation about our efforts. We always find some critics complaining that after-school programs are a waste of money, that mentoring is a failure because some teen killer once was mentored, that at-risk young men in a basketball league use bad language on an outdoor court or that efforts to empower communities are just "outsider" interference.

Waste of money? What about the waste of lives? The cost to society of doing nothing is huge. Increasing graduation rates and reducing violence even a few percentage points brings gigantic savings in everything from prison costs to welfare expenditures. It also provides a better workforce to compete in the global economy and a better, safer community. And can we put a dollar value on lives saved — saved from violent death?

Failure? Sure. Mentoring isn't going to save every kid. For some it won't help at all. A kid could walk from a meeting with a mentor and run right into terrible trouble. That doesn't mean we shouldn't try. Despite critics dredging up some story of failure — as though it was the mentoring that caused an already troubled kid to get in trouble — there are many more stories of success. Statistics show results.

Bad language? A group of at-risk young men might well say more than "gosh" in heated competition on the basketball court. Student-athletes at the very best of colleges and even their coaches have also been known to say something stronger than "gosh" in expressing annoyance at a bad call by an official, a hard elbow from an opponent or a frustrating miss of a layup. To me, the bad language we want to prevent most of all is the gun-wielder's threat to shoot.

Outsider interference? There's not much wrong in "outsider" businesses and non-profits teaming with law enforcement and schools to "interfere" with violence, drugs and gangs in a neighborhood. Neighborhoods sick of violence welcome some attention for once, some resources at last, some opportunity finally for empowerment. Even so, the efforts sometimes are opposed, even sabotaged, by petty local politicians or neighborhood "leaders" who resent the fact that they aren't running the show or being paid to participate.

Chicago, with proof about programs that work, is moving ahead—just as we are in South Bend. Every city with problems of youth violence should move as well. Standing still is too costly.

CHAPTER TEN

Disrespect
"I'm Shootin' Your Ass Off."

WHILE GANGS IN SOME CITIES build arsenals, including assault rifles and other weapons for mass slaughter, most of the fatal youth violence involves the use of handguns. Most of it also involves the word "disrespect" or just "diss" in street lingo.

We can't do much about the availability of handguns for kids who want them. They're everywhere. It's never a problem getting a gun. Even if we got serious about background checks, the millions of handguns that are already on the streets still would be available.

In most of the tough neighborhoods where violence breeds, a gun can be obtained, no questions asked, in street-corner sales. It just takes a little money from drug sales or robberies. Some of the guns are stolen in burglaries. Some are obtained by straw buyers who can pass background checks. They purchase guns from legitimate dealers and then sell the guns to gang members or anybody else with the cash to buy them or something desirable to trade for them. Some come from buyers who go to big gun shows where loopholes permit almost any purchase by almost anybody.

In reporting on how guns flood into Chicago, despite efforts at stricter regulation in that city, the *Chicago Tribune* told of a man who sold four handguns in a South-Side parking lot there and promised the customer he could deliver 24 more in four hours. "Give me $5,000 and you can put your order in then. I'll get you whatever. Give me a list," this gun-runner offered, not knowing he was being recorded secretly by law enforcement. He was going to Indiana gun shows to get the weapons.

So if there is little that can be done now about all those guns already available on the streets, we need to do something about "disrespect."

When I was growing up in Beacon, New York, a small city on the east bank of the Hudson River, we weren't little angels. I confessed in an earlier book that I was involved in a high school prank that got out of hand. As I recall, it seems like a teacher's desk somehow went flying all on its own out a window. OK, not exactly on its own. And I did make sure nobody beneath would be hit.

Beacon was a great place for a kid to grow up in the 1940s and 1950s. But that didn't mean kids never got into fights. We did, usually more pushing than punching, and not resulting in more injury than maybe a bloody nose. The combatants often were back playing baseball or basketball together after differences over some silly disagreement were settled.

It's far different today in the neighborhoods where youth violence is rampant. Now, in a dispute, even over some silly disagreement, one of the combatants is likely to pull a gun. Maybe just to scare. But another combatant is likely also to be armed. Another gun appears. Shots ring out. And there is another young victim of gun violence. When shooting breaks out, innocent bystanders frequently are hit. Or a person presumed safe in a nearby home is struck by one of the stray bullets.

Perceived disrespect—a "diss"—is usually the cause of the gunplay.

Turf...Attitude...Relationships.

Perceived disrespect in any of those three areas of vital importance on the street can bring a violent response.

Somebody walks across the wrong street, invading the turf of a rival gang—a "diss." A warning comes, maybe a warning shot. Repeat offenders face capital punishment, especially if showing the disrespect of selling drugs on the rival's turf.

Somebody is thought to have glared or frowned or showed a hostile attitude in some other way—a "diss." This brings a warning not to be ignored as an idle threat: "Stop dissin' me, you......," or "I'm shootin' your ass off."

Somebody looks too long at somebody else's girlfriend or insults her or makes disparaging remarks about a family member—a "diss." Bullets fired in a gun exchange sparked by an insult to one's mother can lead to something worse than an insult for the mother—the pain of losing her son to death or life in prison.

To curb violence, we must reach these kids. Too late? For some, probably. Unfortunately. That's why we need to reach more of them at an earlier age, in pre-school, in day care, in grade school mentoring or at least in the first years of high school, where we need to stress education rather than just warehousing until drop-out time.

However, we can't just give up on the drop-outs, the gang members, the ones who may already be turning to violence. I refuse to give up on them. We cannot give up on them, for our sake as well as theirs.

We hear misguided grumbling that we should "just let 'em shoot it out" and hope the troublemakers wipe out each other. Really? Just let the bullets fly? And then one stray shot hits you or a member of your family as you drive to the movies or to a sporting event or to the shopping center. Forget about them? And then one of those we want to forget becomes quite memorable with a home invasion. Don't worry about them? And then we are forced to worry about our job force as we compete in the global economy.

I refuse to give up on them for those reasons and also because life is precious. Their lives are important. And in so many cases their lives could be turned around. It's not too late to help some of them turn around their lives. I know. I've seen it happen, helped it happen.

Too many of us are ready to write off any kid who belongs to a gang. There's a big difference between a gang member who affiliates in order to be able to walk safely to and from school and a violent gang-banger.

Jim Brown, the great football running back, wouldn't write off gang members and just "let 'em shoot it out," killing off each other. In 1992, he helped to bring about a truce between the Bloods and the Crips, rival Los Angeles gangs that had been in violent warfare.

As I sought ways to lessen violence in my efforts as director of Operation Weed and Seed, I went to Jim's house in the hills above Los Angeles in September of 1992 for a meeting that was attended by both Bloods and Crips. They were talking, not shooting.

I spotted one tall young gang member who looked familiar. Indeed, he was a former UCLA basketball player. He had joined as a high school kid, doing so for personal safety rather than desire to promote gangbanging violence. All gang members are not the same. Some have real potential for constructive pursuits. Jim sought to appeal to those with potential for something better than death on the streets, those with the intelligence to reach agreement on a truce. He also founded a program called Amer-I-Can to promote self-esteem and desire and determination for success in impoverished areas.

Self-esteem means you don't have to pull a gun when you sense a "diss." You know you can handle things in a better way, a safer way. If you develop desire and determination for success, you won't toss away the chance by shooting over some silly disagreement.

I promoted a basketball league in South Bend as part of the effort to reduce violence in troubled areas. Basketball is a religion in inner-city neighborhoods with predominately African-American populations. That knowledge led to the "midnight basketball" programs that sprang up in the 1980s and 1990s to get gang members in some of the most violent areas to compete with shots on the court rather than shooting in the streets.

The first midnight league was started in 1985 by G. Van Standifer, a town manager in Glen Arden, Maryland, just outside Washington, D.C. The town was experiencing a dramatic increase in violent crime involving 17- to 25-year-olds, so Standifer came up with the concept of getting young men of those ages into a gym to play basketball during the late-night hours when some of them were often involved in real trouble.

Although Republican politicians were later to belittle such efforts as they spread to other cities, it was Republican President George H.W. Bush who brought national attention to the concept with one of his "Thousand Points of Light" awards. He took a helicopter to a game site to praise the effort and honor Standifer. Some of those politicians and talk-radio blabbers contended that the small cost of these programs was something conservatives shouldn't tolerate. President Bush, who appointed me to run Weed and Seed, knew that real conservative philosophy involves giving a boost to volunteer and community efforts that work better than programs run strictly by the federal government. The president was the true conservative.

In Chicago, Gil Walker initiated a highly publicized, highly risky midnight league, with games featuring teams from the crime-plagued public housing projects. Gang members literally had to check their guns at the door. Kind of like in the days of the Wild West, when cowboys had to check their guns at the bar.

There was a draft to pick the best players, so often members of rival gangs wound up on the same team. They learned they could play together, even as teammates. They didn't have to be deadly opponents, reacting to some "diss" over something out on the streets. It would be hard to think the next night of shooting the point guard who got the perfect pass to you for the winning shot.

And it wasn't just basketball. Requirements included attending meetings with black leaders— maybe lawyers or business executives or teachers or plumbers or electricians or carpenters—to hear a positive message about seeking success, not in the National Basketball Association as the next Michael Jordan but as somebody like one of those lawyers, business executives, teachers, plumbers, electricians or carpenters.

Have midnight basketball leagues and other similar leagues been a huge success?

Success? No, not successful at all if you listen to the critics who prop up ridiculous goals, goals never proclaimed or even hinted at by the sponsors, and say: "See, they didn't turn a bunch of young losers into big winners in the NBA."

Huge success? Maybe not, but if a young man decides after doing well in the tough midnight basketball competition that he wants to play just junior-college-level basketball and gets a GED for high school and is admitted to a junior college, isn't that at least some success?

Huge success? Maybe not, but if a young man, who was an excellent high school player but never had grades for college, gets motivated to prepare for college and gets there, even if just a walk-on player who takes classes and takes them seriously, isn't that at least some success?

Huge success? Maybe not, but if a young man

who isn't even very good at basketball, a game he loves, is so motivated to play in the midnight league that he stays out of trouble, becoming not a multi-million-dollar NBA player but a skilled plumber or electrician, isn't that at least some success?

No, midnight basketball isn't a huge success, if the criteria are elimination of violence in the area and turning all the players into NBA stars.

But then, nobody ever claimed it would do that.

The only people who ever suggested that NBA stardom was a goal are critics playing politics rather than seeking to help—like Congressman Lamar Smith of Texas, a giant in establishing the current popularity of Congress. This Mr. Smith went to Washington for "sillyspeak" as exhibited in his rant that midnight basketball is based on "the theory that the person who stole your car, robbed your house and assaulted your family was no more than a disgruntled artist or would-be NBA star."

Clever—but not very.

Make up a theory that a program is aimed at helping some person who has harmed you—like a creep who assaulted your family—and you make cheap political points. Prop up a nutty claim that a program's goal is to discover a great artist or an NBA star, and you can then knock down the claim you invented by showing that no world-renowned artist or new Michael Jordan has burst forth from the program.

Promoters of midnight basketball never claimed

it would end violence or turn gang members into NBA stars. There is no sure cure for violence. Nor is any program or project going to turn all gang members into productive citizens.

What I claim is that we need to do something to help and that getting young men in violent areas to put down guns and put up jump shots is worth a try. Can't hurt. Has helped. We have seen members of rival gangs playing on the same team, working together. If the Bloods and the Crips could call a truce, less notorious rival groups can as well. We know that participating in a real league—with uniforms, coaches, officials and family members watching—is an incentive. It's an incentive to do well, an incentive to avoid troubles on the court or in the streets that could end the chance to participate.

Help is what this is all about. Help for some individuals—and for society. It's not about a magic cure. Not an ultimate solution.

Let's help, I say. Not just with midnight basketball. Let's find other innovative ways to help. Since some areas with growing Hispanic populations have seen problems with the kids joining gangs and getting into trouble, how about a midnight soccer league?

Let's do whatever it takes to capture interest and provide incentives to do something other than hang around on some dangerous corner. Hey, I know of an after-school stamp collecting program that was highly successful.

Let's help the kids, especially those who have guns—or who so easily could get them—to find alternatives to these mad shootings over some "diss" out on the streets.

Richard "Digger" Phelps

Digger shown coaching Notre Dame basketball now uses the same enthusiasm in coaching the streets.

Digger coaching in 1990. In foregroung are three players he cites for their determination to get Notre Dame degrees: LaPhonso Ellis, Tim Singleton and Elmer
Bennett. Singleton, from New Orleans, lost almost everything in Katrina.

Digger gives a pep talk to at-risk youths in the basketball league
he sponsored.

Rev. Theodore M. Hesburgh, while president of Notre Dame, offers encouragement to Coach Phelps. A challenge from Father Ted todo more led to Digger's coaching the streets to do more to help kids.

Digger delivers commencement address at Soulsville Stax Music Academy in Memphis. Emphasis on music there provides the "hook" to get kids to meet high academic standards and graduate.

Digger and Bobby Knight, long time friends as well as coaching rivals, use humor to entertain as well as inform as analysts on ESPN Gameday.

In myriad TV interviews, Digger plugs his causes for improving education opportunities and curbing youth violence.

Digger makes an impassioned plea for mentoring in the South Bend schools.

In an interview at the Superdome in New Orleans, Digger tells of efforts to turn a Katrina-battered high school into a new culinary school stressing college preparation. Louisiana school officials answered his pleas with a $35 million commitment.

To the delight of students at a Soulsville Stax Music Academy, Digger joins the musicians. He praises their academic achievements as well as their rhythm.

Smiles are appropriate for Digger and members of the first high school graduating class at Stax Music Academy. All 51 graduates were accepted for college, with scholarships totaling more than $3.2 million.

Shirley and Walter Collins, whose home was destroyed by Hurricane Katrina, get keys to a new home for their family from Digger. He raised funds to build two New Orleans homes. Shirley and Walter helped rescue victims and then were swept to different locations, neither knowing if the other had survived.

CHAPTER ELEVEN

Respect
"Let's Figure This Out."

RESPECT IS NOT A ONE-WAY STREET. It doesn't flow in just one direction. It must not be demanded but never extended.

Young men on mean streets are quick to pull the trigger over what they perceive as disrespect, a "diss," often over something that most of us would consider relatively minor.

If we are to curtail killing on those streets, we must encourage these young men to show respect—not to respond violently to some "disrespectful" word or glance or other action believed in street culture to require a violent response to prove manhood or ganghood or whatever seems to require proof.

Respect is important, but not in the sense of resorting to violence to demand it after sensing a "diss." It's important for these young men to understand for their own sake that they need to show respect, or at least have the courtesy to listen, when dealing with people who want to help them, who can help them. Teachers are the prime example.

Teachers aren't threatening to pull a gun to demand respect if a potential drop-out won't pay attention in class, won't turn in homework or won't even try to answer questions on a test. Since bad grades don't mean a thing to kids simply waiting for the age when they officially can drop out, there isn't a lot teachers can do. We need somehow to reach these kids to encourage respect for teachers, respect for what the teachers are trying to do, respect for education. We need to convince them that this would be in their own self-interest. They need a high school diploma to find a job that could enable escape from the violent streets. They need basic education skills to hold almost any job these days.

Thinking back to our own school days, most of us can recall some special teacher who really had a positive impact on our lives. We may think of others as well who helped us significantly in our education and in life. If we had paid no attention to them, accorded them no respect, their efforts to help would have been in vain.

Many of these kids never had an adult in their homes that merited a lot of respect. So it's hard to reach them, to convince them that a teacher, a mentor, a coach wants to help and deserves a chance, deserves at least to be listened to.

Many of these kids like sports. That's why a coach can sometimes be the one to reach them, first convincing them it's important to get better grades in order to stay eligible to play and then encouraging them to go beyond that to seek a diploma and consider college or training for a trade.

There has to be some respect shown. If a player won't listen to the coach—won't stop taking bad shots, won't play defense, won't try for rebounds, won't cooperate with teammates—the coach has no choice. The player will be benched or kicked off the team.

I got some front-page attention in the *South Bend Tribune* when I kicked four teens out of the gym for laughing, joking and being disruptive as I talked to players assembled one Saturday afternoon before the games in the basketball league we started for at-risk young men.

I started the league, with games played at South Bend's Kroc Center, as one of the responses to all of those shootings early in 2012. Only 40 kids showed up at the center for the first night of activity in September of that year. Then, as I hoped and expected, interest grew.

By the time I talked to the assembled players early in January of '13, there were 140 there for competition in the league, boys and young men ages 16-24. We already had eight teams and 16 coaches. The players had uniforms. I bought the uniforms and paid for equipment and gym fees. I didn't want those kids going out to raise the money in, well…in some ways we were discouraging. Also, it's important to put your money where your mouth is. Since I've been blessed with many opportunities, I can do that. Unfortunately, many people in South Bend and other communities who have had rewarding opportunities use only their mouths, not their money.

That front-page newspaper article, written by the *South Bend Tribune*'s Jeff Harrell, quoted Leonard Talton, the program's executive director, as telling how the league was "starting to morph."

Said Talton:

> More kids are starting to follow the rules and make adequate decisions. We're moving from making bad choices to becoming more responsible. It's more about being a responsible individual, responsible for your education, responsible for not acknowledging peer pressure when it hits you. Out of these last four or five weeks, not one fight…five weeks and not one fight.

Meanwhile, Harrell wrote, since the last town hall meeting on violence we held at the beginning of the prior summer, there had been only one homicide.

Harrell asked: "Coincidence?"

I told him: "I think it's a combination of everything."

I credited the news media, heightened community awareness, community policing and members of the community "stepping up in their own way."

Well, I was pleased with this initial success, and I wanted that basketball league to work, to help, to save some kids.

And I wanted to talk to the players on that Saturday early in January because my responsibilities with ESPN basketball coverage would be taking me away from home in South Bend. I'd be traveling to basketball courts around the nation rather than being able to get to the Kroc court as often for the games of the at-risk teams. I get home just about every week during the college basketball season, but it's not a long stay so it doesn't permit all of the personal contact and daily involvement of the off-season.

Are some of these players really good at basketball? Yes, really good. The next Michael Jordon isn't out there. But I hope some kid in the league thinks that maybe someday he could be like Mike. Hope is what it's all about. Many of these kids see no hope, no future.

I saw young men with such potential that they could, if they straightened out, play NCAA Division I college basketball. Others certainly, if they got high school diplomas, could play at smaller colleges or junior colleges and, in many cases, get scholarships or other financial aid.

That's why at the meeting I held up a basketball and said: "This basketball is worth $200,000."

Well, a basketball scholarship at Notre Dame was worth that—and actually much more for the future—for Skylar Diggins. In talking to the at-risk kids on South Bend's West Side, I cite Skylar, a kid from Washington High School on the city's West Side, who led her high school team to a state championship and then went to Notre Dame, leading the women's basketball team to three Final Four appearances.

Most of the younger players could at least make their high school teams, maybe as starters, if they stayed in school, stayed eligible and stayed focused on the court. And that could lead to graduation, to that diploma so vital for future success.

"Why don't you deal the ball instead of dealing other things?" I asked.

I try to get across that dealing drugs is controlled by others who make the real profits, while young street peddlers take the risks of violence and/or prison for relatively minor compensation.

Citing Skylar Diggins makes an impression. They know she is a success, already a local legend, because she did things the right way. Skylar is the real deal, never sidetracked in her drive for excellence in the classroom as well as on the court. Skylar became a charismatic national figure as well as a unanimous All-American selection.

Unlike some who forget their neighborhoods and schools and the folks who cheered them along the way, Skylar remembers, and gives back. She will come to talk with and to encourage the kids to persevere, to strive for success.

In promoting mentoring, we invited the mentors

and the kids they are helping to attend a women's basketball game at Notre Dame. Skylar narrated an inspirational message for them that was played during halftime at the game.

Speaking now as a coach—not of the streets but of basketball—and as an analyst of the game, I say with certainty that the Chicago Sky, a team in the Women's National Basketball Association with the No. 2 pick in the league's 2013 draft, blundered in not taking Skylar.

They picked Delaware's Elena Delle Donne, a very good player. And I want in no way to suggest that she was not worthy of being a No. 2 pick.

Skylar, bypassed by Chicago, went in the No. 3 pick to the Tulsa Shock. She will do a great job there for the team and for that city.

My contention that the Chicago Sky made a mistake isn't based on which is the better player. Good arguments can be made either way on that.

But promotion of WNBA teams to attract often-lacking news media coverage and increased attendance is vital in a league with past financial woes and a history of teams folding.

Marketing is important, even for well-known teams in long-established leagues, for crowd size and enthusiasm and community acceptance.

Skylar would have doubled the attendance at Sky games. The throngs of South Bend fans that packed the gym for women's games at Notre Dame, outdrawing many of the men's games, would have thronged as well into Chicago to see Skylar. Tulsa is a little far.

And just think of the marketing mottos: "Skylar reaches for the Sky" or "Sky has no limits with Skylar." Think also of how Skylar would have jumped right in to promote Chicago efforts to curb violence and help at-risk kids. Positive impact. Positive news coverage.

See the Sky? Not now, except when Tulsa comes to town.

Well, getting back to players in our at-risk league in South Bend. They try hard. They want to play. But sometimes they let the street "diss" mentality get in the way.

One kid was thrown out of a game because he was cursing at a referee. He had to apologize to play again. And he wouldn't. I went to talk with him.

"Wait a second," I said. "You gotta go apologize to that guy." He said he wouldn't, couldn't. In the street sense, he couldn't back down from what he considered a "diss" by the referee.

"Let's figure this out," I said. "Who loses in this? You or him? Here we are trying to get your game up to where you could play in college. You can't do that in college. You can't do that with your coach. You gotta understand something. This is not like the streets. You play the street game and the options are jail or dead."

But these kids are conditioned on a way to survive: If you think somebody puts you down, you've got to stand up and fight. You would shoot before you would ever apologize.

I was trying to tell this kid to get above it: "Don't let this beat you. OK, you can be upset. You can be mad. But a bad call won't be changed now. What you said can't be changed now. But you can change whether you get to play again. Get above it. Go apologize." He did. Not immediately. But about five minutes later. So he didn't lose. He won. He played. He responded to a perceived "diss" with a decision showing respect for the game, for the league and for his own best interests.

I threw out those four kids for another lesson. Not for refusing to apologize or back down. But for refusing to listen, to hear whether the message could have meaning for them, and for preventing others from hearing and judging.

"It's all about respect," I told the *Tribune* reporter afterward.

As reporter Harrell wrote:

> Lack of respect is one of many reasons why all of these teens, school drop-outs, and young men were pulled into the "Stop the Youth Violence" mentoring program Phelps initiated last year. Lack of respect for life—the same lack of respect that saw six out of eight gun homicides by May of 2012 involve victims between the ages of 16 and 22.

"Let me have everybody's attention," I asked as I began talking to the league players. As I went on, these four teens were still goofing around, talking to each other and laughing, not listening.

"Excuse me," I said, more friendly than I would have been to any Notre Dame players who ever showed such inattention, such discourtesy. "Did you hear what I just said?"

No, they didn't, and they looked at me as though they didn't care.

"Out of here right now," I ordered. "If you don't understand this, out of here right now. Don't distract from what we're trying to do."

Only four of the 140 young men intending to play that day were kicked out. I hope it sent a message to the 136 still there, ready to play, as well as to the four who lost the chance.

Chapter Twelve

What Parents?
"Raised on the Streets"

WHERE ARE THE PARENTS?

A 16-year-old is shot by a 17-year-old at a gas station at 3 a.m., and folks ask that question: Where are the parents?

When I talk to a group about youth violence, there is the inevitable question: Where are the parents?

I'm tired of hearing that question. It shows a lack of understanding about the lives of so many of the teens who get involved in this violence. There are no parents.

Sure, they had biological parents. But in many of the cases of kids gone wrong, of kids on the streets and involved in violence, no parent is involved in their lives.

I'm not saying that's always the case. There are situations where a single parent or both parents try the best they can to raise a child, only to see the child, despite parental love and guidance, go wrong—go terribly wrong. But there is a pattern of parental absence in the lives of young people who drift through school—no parent there to encourage attendance or homework—and then drop out of school and join gangs, get guns, do and sell drugs and commit violent crimes.

Where are the parents?

Well, if any of those asking the question still think of the American family many of us saw portrayed on television in the 1950s and 1960s in "The Adventures of Ozzie and Harriet," I've got news for them. Many families for many reasons are not like that. They are not like the Nelson family, Ozzie and Harriet and their sons, David and Ricky. There are not always a mother and father married to each other, both in the home, both with the time, resources and interest to raise nice, polite kids who will do well in school and graduate.

In a realistic television show now about the lives of some of the kids who aren't always nice, not always polite, not doing much of anything in school and not likely ever to get a degree, the scenario would be far different than the Ozzie and Harriet portrayal of the ideal American family in the mid-20th century.

There would be no Ozzie. The kids might not even know their father's name. Or if they do, maybe they've never seen him. Maybe a few times, but not since he went away to prison or just went away.

There might be no Harriet on the show. Perhaps she is addicted, off in a crack house or, if lucky, off for help in overcoming her addiction. Perhaps she is long unemployed, off elsewhere in search of a job or off in desperation for money in what is known as the world's oldest profession. Perhaps she has been abused and is off in some new relationship, desperately hoping finally for love. Perhaps she is very industrious, off on three part-time jobs to seek money for the family's food and clothes, even if it means no time with the kids. Perhaps she still hopes to get back in the lives of her kids. For one reason or many reasons, however, she hasn't been in their lives very much, hardly at all.

Who raises a kid in this scenario?

Maybe a grandmother. Maybe an older sibling. Or, too often, maybe the kid is raised on the streets, by the streets.

Some adult in the home, though not a parent, could be trying very hard. Say it's a caring older sister. But she may work part-time jobs, including one at night, so she isn't there to check on a wayward younger brother who won't listen to her anyway.

Being raised on the streets means the cultivation of traits the opposite of what would be taught by caring parents—if they existed. Homework? A joke. Forget it. Graduation? Don't need it. There's more money in pushing drugs than in pushing for some worthless diploma. Listen to teachers? They "diss" you; "diss" them back. Take a nap while they're blabbing. Stay out of trouble? For cowards. Stand up. Seek out anybody who shows disrespect. And take a gun to show you're a man. Never back down.

And it's not just boys raised on the streets. Young girls can be trapped as well in the ways of the streets, wandering about in the dangerous hours after school lets out for the day. They may find a boyfriend providing (or faking) the affection they never knew at home. They may help in gang activities—stealing, pushing. They may conceal guns to be furnished for gang warfare.

Young girls often are victims of violence, caught in the crossfire.

Or they get pregnant, becoming children having children.

Where are the parents?

The reason I'm tired of hearing that question goes beyond just the failure of those asking it to understand that there are no parents in the lives of so many of these kids raised on the streets, by the streets. The question seems to suggest that we can solve the violence problem if we just find where the parents are and force them to be better parents or suffer consequences, like fines or going to jail.

Well, some of them already are in jail. That's part of the problem. We look to putting people in jail as a solution, an easy solution, to all kinds of problems from drug use to shoplifting. That's why we have the highest incarceration rate in the world. How has that worked out? Solved the drug problem? Curbed violence? Turned the jailed into useful, rehabilitated citizens? None of the above?

I learned a lot about the problems of crime and drugs and what does and doesn't work back when I was running Operation Weed and Seed. I think of women I talked with at a Philadelphia homeless center for crack-addicted mothers. Some of them had turned to prostitution to pay for their addiction and wound up in jail. If they had been young corporate executives who became addicted, they could have turned to the human resources director at the corporation and gone off to the Betty Ford Clinic or some other treatment center. They would have been welcomed back, heroes for conquering their problem. The woman at the Philadelphia center and other women in poverty have no chance to go to the Betty Ford Clinic. And if they do overcome addiction, they have no job to be welcomed back to.

Prisons do serve a purpose, but not for everything. Treatment or community-based corrections facilities are more useful for people who are not hardened, violent criminals than are prison cellblocks run by the hardened, violent types.

Send parents to prison for the way they treat their children? Sure, in those cases of horrible, sadistic child abuse. But there is no criminal charge for failure to supervise homework, inability to prevent violent behavior or lack of knowledge about gang affiliation and activities.

We can't pass a law saying you must be a good parent. And even if we could, what would the penalty be for being a lousy parent? Go to jail for not supervising homework or not preventing violent behavior or not knowing a child is involved in illegal gang activity? Sending a parent to jail, especially if he or she is the only parent in a child's life, doesn't make it more likely that there'll be someone who will supervise homework, be able to stop violent behavior or learn about and halt gang involvement.

A parent in prison has no chance at all for parenting.

So, instead of a jail sentence, should we impose fines for being a lousy parent?

Lack of money already is a negative factor in the lives of many at-risk kids. By fining the parent, who may at least be trying to put food on the table and clothe the family, the child is likely to suffer, not be helped. Pay the fine instead of the rent? Homelessness rather than a better home could be the result.

It's easy to point fingers at parents. We should point fingers at ourselves as well if we just harp on the question of where parents are and do nothing to be there ourselves to help the at-risk kids.

Ozzie and Harriett aren't there. However, there

are parents—whether married or single, educated or drop-outs, employed or unemployable—who do love their children and would, if they could, do a better job in raising them for success. They need help. That's why it's vital to have a coordinated effort, to go into high-crime, poverty-stricken neighborhoods with positive programs of help and hope as well as with law enforcement efforts to get rid of negative influences.

Accentuate the positive as well as eliminate the negative. To do this we encourage business involvement—investment, empowerment and providing resources and executive time—as well as participation by schools, non-profits and religious organizations.

We need to help parents, not just ask sarcastically where they were when the kids went wrong. Do they have access to and knowledge of affordable day-care facilities, low-cost housing, help with utility bills, programs for single moms and adult education?

Will all take advantage of this help to improve their own lives and those of their children? Of course not. Some will. Maybe quite a few will. It's certainly worth a try.

But what if it wasn't worth it? What if all of the parents still in the lives of their children in a troubled neighborhood were just plain lousy, not capable of or interested in helping their kids? Just because the parents are a mess is no reason to forsake the children.

If there isn't a caring parent to urge staying in

105

school, there can be a mentor encouraging the kids to set goals for a degree and beyond. If there isn't anyone to see that a child isn't wandering the streets during the danger hours after school, there can be after-school programs more wholesome than the streets. If there isn't an alternative to their gang activity that is apparent to young men, there can be a basketball league or other sports activities to provide that alternative.

If we can't reach the parents, wherever they may be, we still can reach the kids—a lot of them. We can help them. Get them to seek the diplomas most could easily obtain if properly motivated. Get them away from the street violence most would avoid if they could.

Stories abound about such successes. We have the statistics about the programs that work. That's why I'm tired of hearing that question that solves nothing: Where are the parents?

A question that matters is this: *Where are we?*

CHAPTER THIRTEEN

Finding Hooks
"You Can Save a Thousand."

HOW DO WE FIND THE HOOK—the hook on which we can affix a future?

Often it's a hidden hook. I didn't know in college that my future would be with basketball—the hook for a career taking me to the heights of being head basketball coach at Notre Dame for 20 years.

For the young people we seek to help today to find a future better than dead-end prospects on the streets, we encourage them to find a hook, something on which they can hang their hopes and then find success.

When I was growing up in Beacon, New York, as an undertaker's son, and then when I went on to Rider College in Trenton, New Jersey, it was just kind of assumed that I would one day join in the operation of my family's funeral home.

107

This was not a prospect to dread. Not at all. My father, also named Richard Phelps, wasn't just any undertaker. He grew up in an orphanage and went on to become a successful businessman and highly respected member of the community. He and my mother, Maggie, with her deep Catholic faith and Irish sense of humor, were inspirations for me—loving parents who taught respect for others.

Everybody was treated with respect at our funeral home. It didn't matter whether the deceased lived in the affluent or poor part of town, was a big success or was known for failure, was black or white or was Catholic, Protestant or Jew. Clergy of all three of those faiths officiated at Dad's funeral, showing their regard for him.

My dad didn't like cheap caskets. Not because of less profit for him in the sale, but because he wanted no family embarrassed, no deceased deprived of proper respect. He'd pay, if the family couldn't, for an appropriate casket. So, I would have been proud to carry on that tradition, that business, and expand it with a second funeral home, as we planned. Heck, being an undertaker's son even helped me impress girls when I was in college. Really. Of course they didn't know where those beautiful bouquets came from!

My plan was, after getting a business degree from Rider, to go on to Simmons Embalming School in Syracuse, where Dad had learned his profession.

In the summer of 1963, after graduation from

Rider and before heading off to embalming school that fall, I was helping with funerals and had some free time. So, when Tom Winterbottom (the new and successful basketball coach at Beacon High) asked me to coach his Beacon players in a summer league he was starting, I was willing to do that for him. He couldn't coach his own players during the summer under state high school athletic regulations.

I had never thought of coaching. But there it was, a hook on which I was to attach my future. I was hooked, convinced that I wanted to try coaching. So I put off embalming school and went back to Rider for graduate study and the opportunity to be a volunteer basketball assistant. After success in devising game plans there, including one that enabled us to upset New York University, then a national basketball power, on its home court, I was off to gain experience as a head coach. Where? Not exactly at the top.

My first head coaching job was at Junior High School No. 4 in Trenton, not even the power in junior-high play in Trenton. The power was Junior High No. 5, where years later, as Operation Weed and Seed director, I was to accompany Vice President Dan Quayle for an appearance at which the spelling of potato(e) captured national attention. Next in my coaching career was St. Gabriel's High School in Hazleton, Pennsylvania. Then at last, I reached the college level, as an assistant coach at the University of Pennsylvania. That led to the head coaching job at

Fordham University and then my dream job, when I was named head coach at the University of Notre Dame in 1971 at age 29.

If I hadn't found that hidden hook—coaching basketball—my life would have been very different. Not bad at all, I believe, but not nearly as good as the fantastic opportunities I had in 20 years at Notre Dame—the celebrated 1974 win to break mighty UCLA's 88-game win streak, six other upsets of No. 1 teams, regular NCAA Tournament appearances, and our average of just under 20 wins a year.

Let me mention something else important to me, giving me as much satisfaction as the wins. In those 20 years, we had a 100 percent graduation rate and we never had an NCAA violation. So you can see that my concern for education and getting degrees isn't something new.

Now, for me, there's another hook. Thanks to the inspiration and the challenge provided by Father Hesburgh, I'm hooked now on the efforts to coach the streets. We must promote ways to help at-risk kids find some hidden hooks of their own that will lead to better futures.

In Memphis, "Music City," the hook is music. Soulsville Charter School offers music training to attract kids to learn both music and academic skills to enable them to go to college and find success.

In New Orleans, a city known for great food, the hook is culinary. John McDonogh High School will offer an opportunity to learn both culinary and academic skills for jobs, for college, for success.

For many at-risk kids in urban areas—in Chicago, in South Bend and elsewhere around the nation—the hook can be basketball. Chicago has had success in using sports as part of programs to curtail violent crime and increase grade-point averages and graduation rates. The basketball league we started in South Bend after the violence in 2012 has brought results as well.

One example is a young man we'll call "Gary." Gary, like a lot of local young men, goes to the outdoor hoops at Notre Dame for pick-up games. These aren't Notre Dame students. Most will never be students at Notre Dame or at any college. Some, however, are good enough to play college basketball.

Sometimes when I'm out on campus I watch these games. Seems I just can't get away from watching basketball. And I can't stop coaching and giving a little advice—not on technique really. But when I find that some of these young men have no thought of college and have dropped out of high school or plan to quit, I give a pep talk. They listen, most of them, because they've seen me on ESPN and like to hear that I'm impressed with their game.

Gary, a tall point guard who can put on quite a show of basketball skill, was there one day when I stopped their shooting to offer some advice about basketball as a hook for a college education. No way,

Gary thought. He never had played a minute of high school basketball—never even tried out for the team because he "wasn't very motivated" back then. And now he was 24 years old.

I got him involved in the league I started at the Kroc Center. He was a star.

Too old for college?

How about Bernard James? I told him the story of James, who never played in high school after being cut from the freshman basketball team. James enlisted in the Air Force, where he spent six years, serving in Iraq and Afghanistan and reaching the rank of staff sergeant. He played basketball on service teams, and developed skills that convinced him and others that he should give college a try. He did, first for two years at a community college and then for two years as a star at Florida State. He was so good that he actually made it to the NBA, playing for the Dallas Mavericks.

Gary may not make it to the NBA. But why not chase a dream? He could play Division-I college basketball—not immediately, and he knows that. "I can't be greedy," Gary says. "I'd have to start somewhere small. But I'm definitely going to do it."

I'm so proud of him. Gary called me with the great news that he had been accepted at a college and with a basketball scholarship that will enable him to attend. He worked hard on his own for high enough test scores to be accepted at a small school with high standards. He also impressed the coach, getting the scholarship help he needed in order to afford college. He is a soft-spoken young man who can do it, if he retains his present determination. He can play college ball but, most important of all, he can get a college degree, a good job and have a productive future.

Gary's call made it all worthwhile. I'll continue to help him in any way I can. He is, however, doing it on his own now. And I couldn't be prouder of him.

Other young men I'm encouraging to use basketball as a hook for college are still in high school. We'll call one example "Billy." Billy, a high school player with good college potential, was the friend of a kid shot and killed in an incident of teen violence in the summer of 2012. He wasn't involved in the shooting, but a kid doesn't have to be directly involved to be pulled into other violent situations.

Billy went on that fall to be a starter as a junior on a very good high school team. I'm counting on him to stay focused on basketball and school. He can have a future on a college team, with a scholarship and the opportunity for a degree.

Then there is another example we'll call "Joe." I spent a lot of time with Joe, trying to help him. He was in our league at the Kroc Center. He was a good player but really "at risk." And he kept getting into trouble with juvenile crime. I talked to Joe a lot. He seemed like a nice kid who could turn things around if given encouragement and a chance. We got a job for him. And I was encouraging him to get a GED to get into college. Also, I had a college contact for him.

When he got sent to the Juvenile Justice Center after one problem, I went there and chewed him out—just gave him hell—for once again getting into trouble. Also, I got him out. But troubles continued—a probation violation, flunking a drug test, being in a car with some guys with a gun. Still I thought that somehow he would turn things around. He always promised that he would.

As it turned out, he wouldn't. Finally he committed a serious crime that likely, with all of his prior trouble, will send him to prison.

Well, I never claimed we could win 'em all. Sometimes you fail. But with the three examples here, we appear to be winning in two of the three cases. I'll take that percentage or anything close to it. Helping one kid, any kid, is a plus for the kid and the community.

A very wise man named Tony Scott, who has been a school bus driver in South Bend for a quarter century, and who knows all the kids on his route and their problems and potentials, puts it this way: "You save one, and you can save a thousand."

He's right. It's contagious. Violence is. And so is success. An example of achievement—proof of what's possible—can convince others in a community. Those others convince others. It multiplies.

The example of music, culinary skills or sports as a hook that works can convince a lot of kids throughout a whole neighborhood to try for something better than violence.

We need to find the hook. Who knows where it could be hidden? Perhaps one of the kids in our basketball league will find basketball coaching as a hook, just as I did.

CHAPTER FOURTEEN

Funny Thing
"Not How You Throw a Chair"

HUMOR HELPS. It sure did when I was coaching basketball at Notre Dame.

If Tim Kempton, my 6-foot-10 center, missed a layup in practice, I'd holler, "Hey, Timmy, do you need a ladder?" A little sarcastic humor worked better than ranting and raving at players, especially with an intelligent guy like Kempton.

It works also with some of the at-risk kids in the basketball league we started at the Kroc Center in South Bend. After you get to know them and they get to know you, you can joke with them and encourage them to joke back and forth with each other. They need to have fun in competing, not take it in the deadly serious way of competition in a street battle.

Youth violence isn't laughable. Still, in discussing that serious topic, we don't want to become too grim,

117

too depressing, turning off folks who finally throw up their hands and say, "Don't wanna hear about it."

That's why we need to be positive about possibilities and not just negative about what has happened. And add a little humor.

Humor always has been part of my life. I was raised with some humor. It was important to retain amidst the sorrow and grief that an undertaker's family must deal with. In high school, my friends and I would bust each other in the chops—verbally, I stress—in joking back and forth, having fun and building lasting relationships.

One of the funniest things at a serious time, something I still laugh about, occurred when I was director of Operation Weed and Seed and we were trying to get a handle on crime in some of the most troubled neighborhoods right in our nation's capital, Washington, D.C.

I enlisted the help of two young African-Americans, Orlando and J.J. They knew what was going on in the streets and had, in fact, been a part of it. They explained the mind-set of the gangs and the ways of survival on those streets. They knew the territory, and I needed to understand it, too, to help in implementing our Weed and Seed efforts and in reaching the neighborhood residents.

Orlando and J.J. were a tough sell, but I gained their respect. Being known as a basketball coach helped. They told me that to get a better understanding of the mindset I should read *The Autobiography of Malcolm X: As Told to Alex Haley.* They challenged me to read it, thinking that a white guy wouldn't bother. I read it. I got that better understanding, and was enlightened that Malcolm X was not advocating violence.

So, Orlando and J.J. took me "sightseeing" in Washington—to places where tourists would never want to venture. It enabled me to talk with people who otherwise would never have met with me. These young men were guides and also protectors. They could spread the word that "Digger's OK. Not like the others."

After one of our visits to a troubled area, we were running to catch a bus. J.J. was at the street, trying to flag down the bus. Orlando and I were running through a park to catch up, Orlando in front of me. A gentleman on a bench, seeing me running after a young African-American, made an assumption. He called out as I passed: "Good afternoon, officer."

We laughed like crazy on the bus.

We could have sat there expressing anger over the unfair racial stereotyping. But why? The gentleman on the bench wasn't there to hear. Laughing about it—realizing the humor in it—was more productive for us.

Back when I first met Orlando and J.J., their chances for success in the future didn't seem bright. In fact, the length of any future was in doubt—not much longevity on those Washington streets. But they wanted to turn things around.

Both, now in their mid-40s, still live in Washington. J.J. works for the U.S. Postal Service and is proud of his daughter in college. He did turn things around. It was harder for Orlando, who had some real problems along the way. But he now is an electrician and says he is striving to be a good role model for his two teenage sons.

They helped me, a lot, with my understanding of the Washington streets and with my safety. I hope that perhaps I helped them, placing confidence in them and encouraging them. If so, it wasn't through any somber preaching. I didn't do that. But don't underestimate being able to laugh like crazy on that bus about the racial stereotyping. Never underestimate humor. Being able to joke together during serious times can be a help, a tonic.

I could even force a little humor after a big loss in basketball. Hard to think of a bigger loss than losing by 65 points to Bob Knight's Indiana University team in my first year of coaching at Notre Dame. Our roster was depleted through graduation and injury. I even had to borrow three football players from Ara Parseghian. Knight didn't try to run up the score. We were just pathetic that day.

Final score: IU, 94; ND, 29. A friend from New York called after the game to say the wire service had transposed the numbers in the Notre Dame total. He thought the final score was 94-92. "Yeah," I told him, "we lost on a shot at the buzzer." He would find the truth in later accounts. But why go on with the conversation, moaning about injuries, whining about bad breaks, complaining about no depth? Better to play a little joke and have something to laugh about instead of crying about a loss.

Knight is a good friend. Our friendship goes back to our meeting at a basketball clinic when I was a volunteer graduate assistant at Rider College and Bob was an assistant coach at Army. Our friendship continued as rival coaches. We took the competition seriously—and I really enjoyed our victory over IU in Bloomington two years after that 65-point loss "at the buzzer."

Through all of our competition as college coaches, Bob and I were friends, not enemies. We joked with each other. We also had similar principles in recruiting, in requiring players to go to class and in stressing good grades and graduation.

And then there's the chair.

Bob was a great coach. He has the wins and championships to prove that. But throwing a chair in a 1985 game against Purdue gets more mention now than his 1975-76 national championship team that won all 32 games.

We are good friends still as we both work at ESPN during the basketball season. We still joke. Bob long ago began joking about the chair, suggesting that he saw an old lady standing behind the basket and tossed her a chair.

Humor works especially well when you joke about a mistake or mishap in your own life.

Humor works in TV commercials, too. Bob and I were featured in a TV commercial for Applebee's that got a lot of attention during the 2013 college basketball March Madness. It went viral on YouTube.

We were shown eating at Applebee's and watching a basketball game on TV as an announcer describes us as "a couple of retired coaches putting aside their college hoop differences" and enjoying the meal. As the ball swishes the net in the game on TV, I holler: "Yes! In your face, Knight."

Bob says calmly, softly: "You've got anger issues."

I toss over a chair and stomp out.

"That's not how you throw a chair," Bob says, still calm and thoughtful, sipping his ice tea.

Bob was willing to go along with the joke, with a role reversal for him, and with me playing a part viewers would expect him to have.

I guess I should note that I also was known for yelling at officials. But I didn't get many technical fouls. ESPN did research, expecting to find I had quite a few. They were surprised—and I was, too—that they found I had only 11 technicals in 21 years as a head coach.

There was a reason, and it sort of fits in the humor category. When I was up yelling at an official, it wasn't at the referee who made the call I didn't like.

I'd yell at another referee who was close by: "Hey, he's making you guys look bad. That was terrible. But you guys are doing a good job."

I guarantee when they'd go to the locker room at the half, the referee who made the bad call would be asking, "What was Digger saying about me?"

Sometimes I'd end up working all three referees that way. It was a good way to get my views across on how they were or weren't calling charging or other fouls without getting a technical.

Humor can take time. Yep, it takes time to pull a good prank—and to shoot a funny TV commercial.

For the Applebee's commercial, Bob and I flew to Los Angles from Bloomington after ESPN "Game-Day" coverage of the IU-Michigan game. We spent a full day, from 9 a.m. until 6 p.m., shooting takes for a 30-second commercial.

We didn't have a script. They just told us the theme they wanted, and we ad-libbed. I must have thrown the chair 10 times. In one take I asked a guy portraying another customer, "Would you get up for a second, please?" And I threw that chair at Knight. The chair almost hit him! So they toned it down a little in the chair toss.

That was fun. When things aren't fun—and street violence isn't—humor still can help. We can't become so dour and depressed that we can't deal with it.

CHAPTER FIFTEEN

Brazen Gangs
"Counterinsurgency Tactics"

THERE'S A GREAT WAY to encourage kids in elementary and middle schools to avoid gangs and violence. In fact it's G.R.E.A.T.

Those are the initials for the Gang Resistance Education and Training Program. This is a federal program presented in schools by local police officers. The uniformed officers, with training sponsored through the Bureau of Alcohol, Tobacco, Firearms and Explosives (ATF), go into the classroom to talk about gang pressure and violence. They also seek a better relationship between the kids and the police—with better understanding.

Preliminary results from a study of effectiveness showed that the odds of joining a gang were lower for students completing the G.R.E.A.T. program. Those in the program in the sixth grade were 39 percent less likely than control group students to have joined a gang by the eighth grade. We're never going to get 100 percent—maybe not even 50 percent. But even a small percent will be good. And 39 percent is great!

I've worked for many years with Warren S. Harding, Jr., ATF program manager for G.R.E.A.T, to promote the concept. The program now operates in all 50 states.

Harding helped to develop the current 13-lesson program for middle schools, a six-lesson elementary school curriculum, a summer program and a component aimed at parents or other adult authority figures. Though based in Washington, Harding travels around the nation to train local police officers in how to reach kids with a persuasive message about avoiding gangs and violence.

I invited Harding to come to South Bend to talk with the school superintendent, the mayor and the police chief. They gave enthusiastic support. Resource officers were trained, and G.R.E.A.T. was implemented in all of the school system's intermediate centers.

Harding says it all started with a project in Phoenix, where the police and the ATF combined in 1991 to encourage kids to avoid gangs and refrain from violence. Success there, Harding relates, resulted in the concept being implemented in other cities with gang and violence problems. It has been reviewed and revised to adhere to the latest scientifically supported data on effective approaches.

The program is aimed at kids just before the age at which they will in many areas be pressured to join gangs. They are warned about the dangers of gang life—violence, addiction, prison, death—and are taught how to resist pressure and seek more wholesome activities.

Surveys show strong support for the program by teachers and school administrators. Support for having police officers in the schools to present the program was 91 percent among the teachers and administrators surveyed.

Does the program address problems facing the students? Of administrators, 100 percent said "yes." Of teachers, 83 percent said it did.

The kids are shown ways to control anger and resolve disputes without turning to violence. That's important whether or not they join gangs. Also important is an opportunity to see a police officer, friendly and talking sense right there in the classroom, with a positive message in a positive setting. That's far different from the street image of a cop as a bad guy—the image of an enemy to avoid, to hate, or even to kill if needed to avoid arrest.

Seeing cops as friends is a vital part of another program—counterinsurgency, you might call it—in Springfield, Massachusetts. The Naismith Memorial Basketball Hall of Fame is located there. Also there, in Springfield's North End, was a crime-ridden area where gang members ruled, riding on motorcycles

127

with AK-47s strapped on their backs to flaunt the law and show who was in charge.

A riveting CBS "60 Minutes" story told of how Massachusetts state trooper Mike Cutone, also a Green Beret returning from counterinsurgency efforts in Iraq, used strategy aimed at al Qaeda and the Taliban to "pacify" the North End crime territory.

In counterinsurgency tactics in Iraq and Afghanistan, the strategy was for American troops to fight in combat to drive out insurgents and then in peaceful, positive ways to win the hearts and minds of the population. Why not also in Springfield? Certainly more was needed than just police coming in now and then when called to take a report.

Mostly they weren't even called. Crime victims usually didn't bother to report what happened. Why should they? Just to agitate gangs? Gangs ruled and would retaliate. Count on the cops? Police came, if called, but left quickly after finding no witnesses willing to talk, no trust in the community.

Cutone figured that gang members, just like insurgents in Iraq and Afghanistan, "want to operate in a failed area, a failed community or a failed state. They know they can live off the passive support of the community, where the community is not going to call or engage the local police."

He came up with a plan for Springfield—approved, implemented and successful—to send select troopers with special training into the North End's trouble area to challenge the gangs and also to win over the hearts and minds of the people who had had no trust in any cop.

The troopers made clear the turf no longer was owned by the gangs. They walked the streets, knocked on doors and met with the locals in places of business. They also joined with the local police in drug busts and in identifying and jailing gang leaders.

Cutone told CBS correspondent Lesley Stahl about how troopers initially were unwelcome, regarded as useless or racist or just a temporary nuisance. But they kept at it, kept walking and talking, meeting and greeting, all around the neighborhood. Finally, they convinced the population that they were there to help. And just as important, that they were there to stay, not to make a quick publicity splash and then leave.

They started getting tips on who was selling drugs where, who had guns stashed where, who had held up the gas station last night. Calls to police increased. Crime decreased.

They held regular meetings with local residents, representatives of health and housing organizations, business leaders, school officials, local police, political leaders and members of ethnic groups. Coordination.

Coordination is the key—getting everybody together in a coordinated effort.

Coordination was vital with the FBI task forces

that worked with state and local authorities to weed out criminal elements, then worked to encourage community empowerment to keep the criminals out, back when I was director of Operation Weed and Seed.

Coordination of school authorities and police is essential also in the G.R.E.A.T. program.

Determination also is needed. That was especially important in "counterinsurgency" in Springfield. The gang members there were ready to jump right back on their motorcycles with their AK-47s once the troopers left. They were ready to resume drug sales and intimidation of local residents to keep folks from reporting that they had been robbed or had witnessed a killing.

But pressure continued. You can't very well grab your assault rifle and jump on a cycle if you're in jail!

CHAPTER SIXTEEN

Medical Magnet
And a "Crossing"

TOO OFTEN OUR SCHOOLS and teachers are unfairly blamed for youth violence. When we hear of high school kids involved in a shootout or robbery, somebody is sure to denounce their school. "That's a bad school," they say. "No discipline. The teachers don't care."

Yes, some kids from that school did some bad things. But that doesn't make the school bad. How about all the kids getting good grades, taking college preparation courses, winning honors in sports or music, earning scholarships and volunteering in community causes?

I've been critical of the way our education system in America relegates so many students to "remedial" classes when they reach high school, warehousing them, not challenging them. What have we done,

131

however, to reach these kids in the early grades? That's why I push mentoring and after-school programs to try to reach them and help them before they fall behind and drop into those warehousing situations.

Our teachers try. Most do a very good job. And it's a tough job for lower compensation than afforded for lesser responsibilities in other fields. Would you want to teach one of those warehousing classes where it isn't "cool" to pay attention, respect the teacher or try to learn?

Some who complain about a "bad" school (and likely never spent a minute in mentoring or tutoring or any other effort to help an at-risk kid) seem to think teachers should have done something to prevent violence outside the classroom, out on the streets.

Like what?

In South Bend, where I was shocked by teen violence early in 2012, we have some fine high schools, great teachers, and they can't be blamed.

Let me mention one particular high school in South Bend with which I am very familiar and very impressed. It's Washington High School on South Bend's West Side—a part of town that also has some troubled neighborhoods. At Washington, good conduct, proper attire and respect are expected.

And it has become an innovative magnet school for the health care field. That's the hook—just like music can be for that school in Memphis and culinary training can be for that school in New Orleans. Training for health care is the hook that captures the students' attention and encourages academic achievements and desire for success in the future.

Here is the way the school scene was described in a report by Maureen McFadden of WNDU-TV in South Bend:

> A walk down the halls at Washington High might make some feel like they have been dropped on the movie set of NBC's popular and long-running drama "ER."
>
> Students who are enrolled in the school's Medical Allied Health Services Magnet program go to class in scrubs, making it feel like they are walking the halls of ER's fictitious County General Hospital.

The students, coming from various parts of the whole school system, apply for the four-year program. They get on-site training at local hospitals and other medical facilities as well as classroom instruction with professional medical personnel. Some want to become doctors or nurses. Others may be attracted to different employment in the vast, expanding health care field.

Graduates have opportunities to witness operations, see the miracle of birth, observe efforts to save the critically injured from death and be there during medical examinations, both routine and those featuring the high-tech of modern medicine.

They incorporate the medical experience with academics, such as meeting foreign language requirements. As a Washington High School program coordinator explains: "We work hand in hand with their English and their biology and their Spanish [classes]. So when we're doing medical terminology in their courses in health science they may be doing medical technology in their Spanish [class]. They all took medical Spanish because Spanish will give them a leg up in their medical community."

Success in academics in the program is shown by the program's 2012 graduating class earning $2.1 million in financial aid and grants for college. Program graduates won't all go on to become medical professionals, but they will be equipped with academic skills and incentives for success in life. Washington High, by the way, not long ago on state academic probation, advanced steadily and, in May of 2013, was listed as the South Bend high school with the highest graduation rate.

Innovative programs like the medical magnet are needed for high school kids, both for high achievers and for others struggling to find an interest for the future. Also needed, however, are other efforts to make sure we don't lose kids who for one reason or another just don't flourish in our traditional high schools. These often are the at-risk kids we need to reach before they drop out and potentially become perpetrators or victims of violence in the streets.

As I sought ways to tackle violent youth crime in South Bend, I was impressed by the alternative education opportunities that are available.

The South Bend school system operates a nontraditional high school called Rise Up Academy in addition to our four traditional high schools. The academy serves students ages 16 to 21. It's designed especially to help students who haven't kept up with credit requirements for a variety of reasons. Some have dropped out. Others are ready to drop out. Up to eight out of 10 are economically disadvantaged, one of the factors that can lead to problems in a traditional high school.

An important point: The school is NOT for students with severe behavior problems. It is not a reform school.

Another important point: The school is not filled with dumb kids—far from it. Many are very bright. But for some reason, perhaps because of boredom in a traditional school or just not fitting in, they seek something different. They often had attendance problems associated with out-of-school situations, leaving gaps in learning and leading to low grades and failure to meet credit requirements.

At Rise Up, classes are smaller, enabling more individual attention from teachers. Students often had felt out of place or ignored in the larger classes at their traditional schools. In addition, schedules are more flexible, with on-line learning outside school offered, allowing older students with part-time jobs or students with children to continue their education.

Rise Up actually was about to go down in 2011. It was on academic probation for five years—the limit before state intervention to take it over. Most of the problems went back to operations at a different location, with inadequate staff, poor planning and questionable selection of the students for this type of schooling.

A new principal, George Azar, determined and innovative, with a new staff and at a new site, set higher standards.

Results: Test scores at the end of the 2011 school year went way up, more than doubling what the state required. No state takeover. No more probation. No more looking down on this school.

Here is more proof for my contention that kids will meet the challenge if expectations and goals are set higher. Set grade standards higher for participation in sports or band or yearbook and it provides a hook for kids who want to take part in those activities. They will do better academically in order to participate. Give them a challenge to improve their school's academic standings or see their school taken over by state outsiders and they come through on state tests.

Unchallenged kids obviously can't meet a challenge never provided.

Rise Up is living up to its web page motto: "We are the Phoenix—building academic excellence and self-empowerment in a supportive culture." Schools like this are needed to provide an opportunity for students to rise up after falling down in and/or dropping out of traditional schools.

Private alternative schools also offer opportunities. In South Bend, I'm impressed by the Crossing Educational Center, a private, faith-based alternative school. Crossing includes actual job training along with academic courses that can lead to employment after graduation.

Getting a job is vital for many of the young people who turn things around and get a high school degree after dropping out or falling behind. Not all will go on to college. And many of those who want to pursue a college education will need a job to afford higher education.

Working with Rob Staley, CEO for the Crossing facilities in South Bend and other sites in Indiana, I've referred a lot of kids there and have been impressed with their success in obtaining diplomas and jobs. Staley stresses on-the-job experience, where students (before graduating) join work teams, spending half of their school day in class and half on a job—good jobs, not those at the lowest rung.

Also, they can earn Ivy Tech Community College credits on those jobs. That's a start for college—an incentive for college. Ivy Tech offers degrees or certificates in everything from accounting to nursing, from automobile technology to computer science.

At the Crossing, where it's understood that many of the students had troubles in traditional schools due to poor attendance, stress is on getting to class and to those part-time jobs. Failure to show up means failure. It's just not tolerated.

One of the many success stories I know involves a kid—we'll call him "Mike"—who was kicked out of high school and was jailed twice, once on a very serious conviction for shooting at another kid at a mall. Mike is a loser. Right? Well, he could have been lost. But Rob Staley gave him another chance at Crossing, with the faith-based component important there. Mike started reading the Bible, a book offering a different direction than the street bible's golden rule: "Shoot unto others before they shoot unto you." He wanted something better than the direction in which he had been headed—a place called oblivion.

Mike got his high school degree from the Crossing Center at age 19—a little older than the usual high school graduate, but also wiser than many other graduates.

As he left with his diploma, Mike had a full-time job and was going to Ivy Tech for college study as an x-ray technician. I talked to Mike to congratulate him. Also to give him a pep talk about staying on course for a place other than oblivion. Mike, before being kicked out of high school, had been a basketball player. He loves and follows the game. And Staley told me that Mike was startled that the ESPN basketball guy would follow his progress and offer congratulations. Staley said he offered another challenge to Mike: "Digger is going to mention your story in a book." In other words, don't mess up a good story by messing up. I'm hoping Mike will do well. I think he will.

Students who impress the employers in their on-the-job education, as Mike did, often are hired by those employers after graduation. Or at least their favorable recommendations help the students in finding jobs elsewhere. Employers who get to know and respect the work ethic and ability of these students will hire them, despite some delay in graduation or mistake in life that might otherwise have caused rejection.

We don't want an at-risk kid, who stumbled somewhere on the streets but turned things around, to face unemployment, discouragement and entanglement again on the streets. This is where the business community must step up, step in. In South Bend, I was able to find employers who would give a chance to some of the young people I coached on the streets—coached off the streets. These kids need jobs. And businesses need them.

While unemployment has remained high, there is the seemingly contradictory fact that many companies have openings but just can't find qualified applicants to fill them. Well, institutions like the Crossing Center and Rise Up will provide qualified applicants. The business sector needs to hire them, not write them off merely because a résumé shows it took them an extra year or more to get a degree.

Now, with global competition, with our economic future at stake, we cannot afford to keep pushing so many kids into warehousing classes and then writing them off if they drop out. Get them back in, into a Crossing or Rise Up, and then, if they strive successfully for a degree, give them a chance to show they can contribute to our workforce. They deserve the chance. And the workforce needs them.

CHAPTER SEVENTEEN

Dream Team Mentors
And Students "Giving Back"

MENTORING HAS BEEN A CAUSE for me since my days of directing Operation Weed and Seed, where I saw the success of a program in the San Antonio school system, with military personnel stationed in the area doing a great job of working with at-risk kids. We knew that once we weeded out the bad elements, we needed positive programs to keep the weeds of gangs, drugs and violence from flourishing again.

So, back in South Bend, I helped to organize what I called the Dream Team Mentoring Program. Everybody was still talking about the U.S. 1992 Olympic "Dream Team," winners of the gold medal in basketball. Well, why not a "Dream Team" to win at home for kids in need of some guidance from a caring adult?

"I don't want your money. I want an hour." That's what I tell prospective volunteers.

The program requires only a commitment to meet for an hour each week during the school year with a youngster needing somebody to listen and care. It's important for children in the early grades. That's when some kids, especially those with no adult figure showing concern for them at home, truly become at risk.

They need somebody to talk to about their interests, their hopes, their fears—not just about arithmetic or English, but about problems in their lives that could rob them of self-esteem or become a source of anger. They will talk when convinced that there is somebody who cares about them and is willing to listen.

Studies show that mentoring works—and it works particularly well with disadvantaged kids. Quality mentoring was shown to make these kids more likely to develop a positive attitude toward school, less likely to skip classes, more likely to go on to graduate and less likely to get involved in drugs, alcohol and violence.

In the 18 school years I've been involved in promoting the mentoring program, I've heard countless stories of success. As communication and confidence develop, mentors can provide not only positive advice and encouragement but also contacts in areas of the student's interests. This can help in later decisions on educational choices and the selection of a future career. It also can lead to a part-time job or internship.

The child may tell the mentor about some problem never mentioned to a family member. Maybe there is no family member who cares. Often there are solutions that can be found.

And it's not just the kids who benefit. So do the mentors. When a mentor sees a youngster developing confidence, making the right decisions and expressing positive attitudes about education, there is no way to put a dollar value on that. You see that your investment in time actually has made a difference.

You're coaching this youngster in the game of life. And when the youngster wins, you are a winning coach. It's like the way it was when you woke up on Christmas morning and found a great present you didn't expect. You're surprised about it—also elated!

When a positive relationship is developed, the youngster is not going to forget. Mentors tell of the thrill of being invited to a kid's high school graduation or hearing from the kid who was mentored about how things are going in college. If you had not been involved, would there have been a high school diploma or college attendance? Maybe it wasn't only through your efforts. But you can be proud that those efforts helped at a critical stage.

Sometimes prospective mentors beg off because of parental responsibilities with their own children. Yes, their own family understandably comes first. However, mentors have said that listening to and understanding the concerns of another youngster has made them better parents—or better grandparents.

It also broadens the perspective of the mentors. It

gets them out of their own "bubble," where they live and work and attend events with people much like themselves. It gives them an understanding of life in different circumstances in different parts of town.

We are fortunate in South Bend to have available the most important resource at the University of Notre Dame—the students. Community service and "giving back" are stressed at Notre Dame. Students help a lot with tutoring. One off-campus Notre Dame facility that does an outstanding job is the Robinson Community Learning Center, operated in partnership with Northeast Neighborhood residents.

They have an amazing Shakespeare program. Young people from the community as young as eight years old get to know the works of Shakespeare. They put on a full-length play in the spring. Actors, including those in older divisions extending through high school, can participate in a monologue competition on campus sponsored in the fall by Shakespeare at Notre Dame. There also is a five-week summer camp opportunity for the participants.

The Notre Dame students benefit, too. Many of them are from communities around the nation where they had little or no contact with disadvantaged and at-risk kids. They get to see a part of "the real world" that they want and need to understand.

One student who was tutoring a third-grader at Robinson told of amazement at hearing this little kid reciting Shakespeare, accurately and with pride in the achievement. And they don't just memorize. They understand it. This shows the potential that young kids have and how they will meet the challenge. What a shame it is when we don't seek to develop the potential and fail to provide a challenge.

The Dream Team Mentoring Program has taken advantage of university proximity by taking the program participants to Notre Dame women's basketball games. Although these youngsters live close to the Golden Dome, many of them never have set foot on campus before. They get to see a college and something of college life. They could start thinking that perhaps someday, if they take education seriously, they could be college students—even college graduates—with greater opportunity for success in employment and in life.

Would they think about college if they had never seen one? Could they picture themselves in college life if it was all something foreign to them?

As I noted earlier, the starring role of Skylar Diggins on the women's basketball team provided incentive to strive for success. All the kids had heard of her, had seen her on television and know that she grew up in South Bend, too, leading her high school team to a state championship and then becoming an All-American at Notre Dame.

Notre Dame students certainly are not the only college students who can help in combating the problems of at-risk kids and violence in the streets. In fact, other colleges in South Bend—Saint Mary's College, Indiana University – South Bend, Bethel, Holy Cross and Ivy Tech—all have students volunteering for community projects.

Every urban area with at-risk neighborhoods and trouble in the streets has some college nearby. That is a resource to be tapped in all those areas. On every campus, there are students willing to help, anxious to help and able to reach disadvantaged kids that really are not that much younger than they are.

CHAPTER EIGHTEEN

The Motto
"Don't Assume It Can't Be Done."

Don't assume.

Follow up.

Always have a backup.

That was the motto for success that I posted in the Notre Dame locker room. I had other messages for the players, such as a sign with the advice:
"To be successful:
(1) Listen.
(2) Talk to each other.
(3) Concentrate on each situation."
But the "don't assume" admonition is what seems to be remembered most. That's probably because I preached that advice beyond the locker room. It was not just advice for players in a game. I viewed it as advice for success in life. And I told the players, hey, this was advice that would hold true for success

147

after graduation, for after playing days were over, for out in the world. I preached that motto to assistant coaches, trainers, team managers, secretaries in the basketball office—and beyond.

I ran into Brooks Boyer, who played on my last Notre Dame team, at a Chicago White Sox baseball game. I was there to see my son-in-law, Jamie Moyer, then with the Seattle Mariners, pitch that day. Boyer by then was marketing director for the Sox.

In greeting my former player, I jokingly rattled off: "Don't assume. Follow up. Always have a backup."

"Coach, follow me," Boyer said. "I've got something to show you in my office."

From a cabinet behind his desk he pulled out an old piece of paper going back to his first day as an intern in Chicago sports, for the Chicago Bulls. Written on it were the words: "Don't assume. Follow up. Always have a backup."

In an interview with the *Chicago Tribune* after Boyer had become vice president in charge of marketing for the White Sox, he told of how he realized after playing college basketball that so many other players were so good that he couldn't make it in the pros.

"My backup plan," he said, "was to find a way to get into the sports business."

He found it when he went to a Bulls game to see his former Notre Dame teammate LaPhonso Ellis, who was there as a member of the Denver Nuggets.

148

Boyer met the Bulls marketing director. They talked about his interest in the sports business field, and that led to Boyer being offered an internship with the Bulls right after graduation.

A year after impressive work as an intern, Boyer was a full-time marketing assistant for the Bulls. Jerry Reinsdorf, owner of both the White Sox and the Bulls, then moved Boyer to marketing chief with the Sox the year before they won the 2005 World Series. He also is chief executive officer for another Reinsdorf enterprise, Silver Chalice, operating digital-based businesses in sports, media and entertainment.

By the way, Brooks didn't just display my motto for success to humor his old coach. When asked during a 2007 interview with *Sports Business Daily* what business advice he would give, he cited…well, you guessed it, that very motto.

I try to give examples of what I mean by citing airline travel. Don't assume seats will be available, flight schedules remain the same or anything else about the flight. Find out. Then follow up. If you've decided, act before the seats you want, aisle or window, are gone and prices go up. Most important with air travel, at least for me in taking planes so often in the winter to and from South Bend, is always have a backup.

With plane travel for my Notre Dame team, I insisted on a backup plan, and it often was needed. Say we were flying out east and had a stop in Cincinnati.

What's the weather forecast for Cincinnati? If it's a heavy snow warning, a wise backup could be travel instead through Detroit. And where is the connecting flight coming from? Could bad weather ground it there? How about the return to South Bend? The words "heavy lake effect snow warning" could mean a backup plan for bus transportation from Chicago. *Always* have a backup.

That motto can be good advice in so many areas—in employment, in sports, in personal relationships, in life.

Another list I often cited to players and to just about anybody else who would listen is of the qualities of leadership. For leadership, I would say:

(1) You gotta be creative.

(2) You gotta be a risk taker.

(3) You gotta have street smarts.

(4) You gotta know how to be a survivor.

Think about it. Most good leaders are creative and have taken risks to make it to the top.

By street smarts I mean knowing more than book smarts. Of course there's nothing wrong with book smarts. I spent 20 years at Notre Dame urging my players to hit the books. And I crusade now for at-risk kids to get good grades and diplomas. But leaders must also know the territory, know the people they seek to lead, know what's happening and what can be done about it in that territory, that city or in those streets.

Be a survivor? Yes, leaders often have been tested—knocked down, pushed out, held back. How many stories are there about some successful person who was fired from a first job? They have to be able to survive the adversity and push on with determination.

Think of something else as you look back at that list. Those are qualities you could find, though with different purposes, in gang leaders. They are creative. Unfortunately so, whether it's creating a drug distribution system or a protection racket. They certainly are risk takers. And they have to know how to survive.

The street-smarts bit is a little different. They're not using their smarts for the good of everybody on the streets. Their smarts lead to bad things when they find ways to intimidate and recruit other gang members, sell more drugs, obtain more weapons and shoot more victims.

What a shame, however, that these gang leaders and other gang members with some of the qualities of leadership are leading in the wrong direction. Could we turn some of them in a different direction? It would be difficult. Yet, it has sometimes been accomplished. Jim Brown worked with gang leaders for a gang truce in Los Angeles. Some gang leaders have turned to anti-violence causes. They have become effective spokesmen. Only a few successes can save many kids.

Don't assume it can't be done.

My motto works in combating youth violence.

Don't assume. Most of all, don't assume that at-risk kids can't be helped; that the situation is hopeless; that we'd somehow be better off to let violence take care of itself, with shootings serving a useful purpose of trimming gang ranks. And don't assume that the problem can be handled by somebody else— the police or teachers or government officials. The community, with individual volunteers and business involvement, is needed to help police, teachers and government. They need help from neighborhood-watch groups, mentors and volunteers for programs for which tax money is not available.

Follow up. Good intentions are of little use if they aren't followed up with action. Don't just think about maybe being a mentor, do it. Don't just grumble about crime in the neighborhood, join a neighborhood watch. If you run a business, don't just complain about lack of qualified employees, support efforts of alternative schools to turn out capable graduates. Don't just lament that some public officials stand in the way of efforts to help at-risk kids and curtail youth violence. Don't just holler about it, go to the polls to defeat them.

Always have a backup. That's important, whether dealing with bad weather when travelling or bad results from a seemingly useful plan or program to deal with youth violence. Not all of those plans and programs will work everywhere.

In this book, I seek to present a smorgasbord—a lot of choices for dealing with the problem. There is no one sure cure.

What works in one community may not work in another. We need to tailor programs to communities—music as a hook for at-risk kids in Memphis, culinary for New Orleans.

A plan successful in one city could fail in another for a variety of reasons. Failure could be due to public apathy, lack of adequate funding, poor planning for that community's needs and interests, opposition from local officials or the school board, or disinterest by local businesses.

If midnight basketball isn't the answer for at-risk kids in a troubled Latino neighborhood, how about midnight soccer?

A neighborhood-watch group could go astray—more vigilante than vigilance. Thus, it could do more harm than good.

The purpose of this book is to present possibilities—not dictate what must be done. I want to offer that smorgasbord of what has been done in Memphis, New Orleans, Chicago and elsewhere.

If we have 20 choices, something is likely to work. Decisions need to be made neighborhood by neighborhood, city by city, state by state. The people need to find them. The politicians may not.

Don't assume it can't be done. Follow up if you can help. And always have a backup.

CHAPTER NINETEEN

Boston Strong
"Isn't the Reaction that Terrorists Want"

"**WE'RE GOING TO WIN.**" A coach must convince the team of that.

No team wins 'em all, of course. But going into a game with a defeatist attitude almost guarantees a loss. Going into the toughest of games with confidence can help to bring victory.

So it was with coaching basketball.

My Notre Dame basketball teams were convinced they were going to win when we upset seven No. 1-ranked teams.

Heck, in the biggest upset, when we beat UCLA and coaching great John Wooden, the legendary "Wizard of Westwood," ending their amazing 88-game winning streak in 1974, my players already had practiced cutting down the nets. To build

155

confidence three days before the big game, I told them they would be cutting down the nets in celebration and they ought to know how to do it with style on national TV after our victory.

In our 1977 upset of San Francisco, a No. 1 team coming into Notre Dame with a 29-0 record, we had our students clapping to a rhythmic chant of "twenty-nine and one, twenty-nine and one." Our students in the stands and our team on the court were convinced that would be our opponent's record after the game—and darned if it wasn't.

See what I mean about how important it is in basketball coaching to build confidence?

So it is also with coaching the streets.

We're going to win.

When I returned home after the 2012 NCAA Final Four and saw that shocking *South Bend Tribune* headline about the spike in youth violence—about five young people shot in three violent incidents—I knew we had to do something. We couldn't keep losing lives. We had to win.

When I came up with that game plan for action and recruited key players for a "Stop Youth Violence Team," my goal was to build community confidence in the idea that we could make a difference.

When I saw the enthusiasm at our town hall meeting, with nearly 700 concerned folks ready to help, found that neighborhoods were coming together to combat violence and observed at-risk kids responding to the opportunity to compete on a basketball court rather than on the streets, I knew we were going to win. And darned if we didn't.

After the violence in April, with all signs pointing then to a long, hot summer of killings, we had a cool summer—not violence free—but nothing like the violent spring. While homicides were up in 2012, due mainly to that bloody start, by the end of the year, police reported a 20-percent overall drop in crime.

Just as in basketball, no team wins 'em all. But every win on the streets means a lot—a lot of lives. Police credited community involvement in helping to lower the crime rate. The officers themselves deserve a lot of credit. They virtually wiped out one violent gang with arrests that brought prison sentences.

South Bend police—through questioning informants, scouring social media sites and finding links in a series of youth violence incidents—identified 29 members of a gang calling itself the "Cash Out Boyz." The Boyz actually bragged on Facebook.

What started as at-risk neighborhood kids getting into trouble on the streets grew into what authorities called a bloody criminal enterprise involved in homicides, drug dealing and armed robberies. South Bend police in a coordinated effort with county, state and federal law enforcement personnel and prosecutors began to crack down on the gang. Arrests. Convictions. Prison.

In April of 2013, the last known member of the gang still free on the streets was arrested with community help—a tip to Crime Stoppers.

They all were locked up—most already convicted on charges up to and including homicide. Good news.

In another sense, it was sad news, too. Most were ages 16 to 19 at the height of their violent activity. Some had records of getting in trouble as early as age 10. So, yes, it's sad that these kids did things to ruin their lives, take other lives and cause such pain for so many of their victims. Was there something that could have been done to save at least a couple of them and save the community from some of that pain? If so, something had to be done earlier in their lives.

But it was too late now. So police, doing their job well, came in to win that battle for control of the streets.

While there were many neighborhood groups helping police to win that control, one with a rather unusual name was especially effective. They call themselves the "Diamond Divas."

The ladies in this neighborhood-watch group in the Diamond Avenue area of South Bend got fed up with the violence. A while back their neighborhood became one of the worst crime-infested areas in the city—crack houses, street-corner drug sales, burglaries, armed robberies, shots fired throughout the night, as well as homicides.

These brave ladies started going out with cell phones in hand, patrolling the streets and standing on the corners known for drug sales and violence. They'd call police when trouble brewed or illegal activity was viewed.

Some at-risk kids who knew the ladies and knew they meant business stayed away from the trouble spots. There were gangbangers, however, who decided to scare the watchers, walking by the ladies with threatening gestures and displaying their guns. The divas didn't scare.

Well, the gangbangers apparently realized that shooting a defenseless middle-aged woman would be kind of hard to brag about as a macho act of bravery. So they moved their criminal activity a few blocks away. With the sound of shots coming from a new location, the divas walked in that direction. They didn't walk home. They didn't run away.

The Diamond Divas won.

The city made street improvements on Diamond Avenue. The gangbangers fled in fear of the divas or were taken care of by the police. The neighborhood now is safer, nicer. And the Diamond Divas still keep watch to keep it that way.

Other neighborhood groups sponsored picnics and other activities for kids as school started in the fall, giving support for education and sometimes giving backpacks and school supplies to help the kids get off to a better start.

A year after that newspaper headline about youth violence in my own town, I was back home again in South Bend after the 2013 Final Four, feeling better about what had been accomplished. I do think we made a difference.

Then came new headlines—not about South Bend, about Boston. These headlines told of a different type of violence, terror at home to promote hatreds arising from afar: The bombs at the April 15, 2013, Boston Marathon.

Fewer died there than in youth violence in South Bend—and nothing like the Chicago toll—but there were hundreds of terrible injuries and there was the intent to injure the entire country.

Even though one of the accused bombers was just 19 years old, this was something far different from our type of youth violence. The bombs at the marathon finish line weren't exploded to establish gang turf or to retaliate for a "diss" by some rival. They were intended by radicalized attackers who grew up in our midst to terrorize us, to show that no place is safe. If security isn't secure at an iconic event like the Boston Marathon, right at the finish line in the focus of national TV, where can there be safety?

Boston and the rest of the nation, however, did not respond by cowering. Medical personnel, security officials and runners who were just finishing a 26-mile race didn't flee but instead rushed to the bomb scene, helping to save lives.

The motorist whose car was hijacked by the accused bombers didn't just cower in fear as he heard them brag about what they had done and what they would do. When he saw a chance to escape, he ran for his life and lived to alert authorities to the identity and location of the suspects.

Boston Red Sox fans showed no fear of going on with their lives as they packed Fenway Park for the first game after the bombing. They cheered the police. They cheered marathon volunteers and runners. They cheered the medics and other first responders. They cheered for the USA. And a "B Strong" logo adorned the Green Monster—the high leftfield wall at Fenway.

Neil Diamond called to say he was in town and wondered if they would want him to sing live his song played at every Red Sox game, "Sweet Caroline." Yes. Of course.

That song, identified with the Red Sox, was played as well at Yankee Stadium, where solidarity with Boston is inconceivable in terms of baseball. But the solidarity of the cities, of the nation, after the bombing attack was proclaimed proudly as Yankee fans sang the Red Sox song.

One particular stanza of "Sweet Caroline" took on special significance:

> And when I hurt,
> Hurtin' runs off my shoulders.
> How can I hurt when I'm with you?

Warm, touchin' warm
Reachin' out, touchin' me, touchin' you.
Sweet Caroline.

A passionate speech was delivered by David Ortiz, the Red Sox baseball star. They call him "Big Papi." He dropped what some would describe as an "f-bomb" in expressing his determination to stand "Boston Strong." Profanity? Nobody cared. The real profanity was the bombing, not anything in his passionate remarks.

Even the chairman of the Federal Communications Commission brushed off usual FCC concern with such language being broadcast, saying Ortiz "spoke from the heart" and adding: "I stand with Big Papi and the people of Boston."

Yes. And Americans not only stand with Boston, they will run again in Boston, in that marathon. Planning goes on for bigger and better races.

Polls conducted soon after the Boston bombings showed Americans determined to go on with their lives and not surrender to the fear that terrorists seek to spread.

A Fox News nationwide poll found that the bombings had sparked more anger than fear. When asked which best described how they felt about the bombings, 58 percent picked "angry," more than double the 27 percent saying "worried." More than eight out of 10 said the terror in Boston won't change how they lead their everyday lives. And nearly seven in 10 expressed confidence that their community is prepared to handle a terrorist attack. That was up from just 47 percent in 2006. So confidence actually was going up, not down.

A *New York Times*/CBS News poll found 84 percent approval for the way federal and local law enforcement authorities handled the Boston bombings. Americans also are realists. That poll also found that nine out of 10 acknowledged that they will always have to live with the threat of terrorism. But 72 percent said they did not plan to avoid large public events to reduce possible exposure to a terrorist attack.

The determination to go on with their lives didn't mean that they wanted nothing to change. They overwhelmingly supported installing more video surveillance cameras in public places. Most expressed confidence that the government can combat terrorism effectively through rigorous law enforcement and proper regulation.

Confidence. Determination. Being more angry at terrorists than being terrified of them. This isn't the reaction that terrorists want.

We're going to win against terrorism, just as we're going to win in our efforts to reduce youth violence— although not every time, every day, every year.

There will be other terrorist attempts. The vast majority will be stopped—probably not all.

There still will be kids killing kids on the streets. We will significantly reduce the toll—though not to zero.

That's winning—winning BIG in two of our toughest battles.

CHAPTER TWENTY

New Opponent
"Have the Courage."

WE'RE GOING TO WIN. My doctors and I are going to win in another challenge against a tough opponent: Cancer.

Back at home in South Bend after the 2013 NCAA Final Four—a year after rampant youth violence prompted me to form a team to fight that violence—I was diagnosed with bladder cancer. Now, my doctors, my family and I are a team to fight the cancer.

Tough opponent? Yeah, but not unbeatable. I beat cancer once before with successful surgery for prostate cancer back in June of 2010.

Early detection was important then. Early detection and the immediate start of treatment will lead again to a win for modern medicine, for great doctors, for my family and for me. The prognosis is good. This cancer is not related to the earlier prostate cancer. No spread was found elsewhere.

There is no defeatist attitude for me. Not after all the years of preaching confidence in victory to my basketball teams, to our community team confronting youth violence and to people involved in every other cause in which I've been involved. Not after all the love and support I receive from my family and friends. Not after the blessing and call for courage from a man I have regarded as a living saint.

Tough game? Think win. Practice cutting down the nets.

I have been preaching about the value of regular physical exams and early detection of medical problems.

When I turned 60, I decided to have a physical examination twice a year instead of just an annual physical in October. Being an undertaker's son, I saw what causes death when undetected for too long and treated too late. I also saw how frequently some hardworking guy would retire, seemingly in good health, but then just do nothing—no activities, no interests, no attention to health—and be dead in a year.

What if I sailed through an October physical trouble free, but something kicked in that November? There'd be a long wait until the next annual physical. So I added another physical in April, right after basketball season.

In the April exam in 2010, the prostate cancer was discovered. As soon as I knew the extent of the problem and the type of treatment recommended by the doctors, I was all set for action. I freely admit, however, that the time awaiting the biopsy evaluation was a living hell. It's the unknown. You don't know what they're going to find. How bad is it? Thanks to early detection and quick treatment, it wasn't that bad, that advanced. After da Vinci robotic-assisted surgery, I was cancer free. By the time of an October exam, if cancer had not been found and treated in the spring, who knows where it would have gone?

I became a spokesman for efforts to encourage men over 50 to get examined. There is dispute now in the medical field about who should get the PSA test and when. The best advice is to get a regular medical exam and talk over testing with the doctor—then follow the doctor's advice. And, if treatment is recommended, be aggressive—don't delay.

Men are notorious for neglecting exams and putting off going to the doctor when they begin to suffer symptoms of physical disorder—kind of a macho thing. They think they're supposed to be super beings. No, just human beings. Don't put off seeing a doctor and following medical advice. Get it done.

That, of course, is good advice for women, too. We know the value of early detection and treatment of breast cancer.

Again, it was my April exam that led to the discovery of the bladder cancer in 2013. I had thought that some blood in the urine was just from a blood thinner I was taking to prevent heart attacks and strokes.

There was a tumor. It was taken out. It was small, but it was malignant. So, more treatment is required. No spread of cancer was found, and treatment is designed to make sure that continues to be the case.

Early detection and early treatment are again on my side.

Fear of the unknown was there again, of course. Then you find out: OK, here's what it is. And here's the game plan to go after it. Let the game begin.

Different type of game. Yet confidence of winning still is important.

I'm always amazed by the techniques of medicine. My treatment to reduce the risk of cancer returning will involve injecting BCG (Bacillus Calmette-Guerin) vaccine into the bladder. It's a tuberculosis vaccine originally used to treat TB. Why it works in bladder cancer treatment is a mystery to me—and I guess to doctors, too. But it works. It appears to stimulate the immune system to destroy any remaining cancer cells.

The treatments will go on for two years, with more frequency at first and then every six months in the second year.

I also believe in prayer. So I visited "the hidden crucifix" in the woods near the lakes at Notre Dame. Tourists and football fans coming for the games don't see it. It's out of the way, not really famed as is the

Grotto. The cross is on a mound in the midst of the woods, with statues of Mary, the mother of Jesus, on the right side and Mary Magdalene, surely an Apostle, on the left. This is one of the most spiritual places on campus. And, of course, I went immediately to see Father Hesburgh to ask for his blessing.

Early in this book, I told of the role of Rev. Theodore M. Hesburgh in my life, from coaching basketball at Notre Dame to coaching the streets. Father Ted, the longtime president of Notre Dame, was the man with the final say when Notre Dame hired me back in 1971. He provided inspiration and guidance in my years of coaching and beyond. His challenge to me to do more after coaching than be an ESPN analyst during the basketball season is why I made a commitment to coach the streets, to do more to help kids needing help.

I am a Hesburgh disciple. What Mother Teresa was to nuns, Hesburgh is to priests. The man is a saint.

He always seems to have just the right words. After we talked and he gave his blessing and I was ready to leave to confront this new cancer, he told me: "Have the courage."

And I kept thinking about that advice, really words of inspiration to take the challenge, to have the courage to fight to find a way to win.

"Have the courage."

I will.

My doctors have given me a winning game plan for defeating this cancer. We're going to win. After all, I've got a lot more streets to coach. And we're going to win out there, too.

A Smorgasbord

I'VE TRIED TO PUT MANY CHOICES on the table for communities facing problems of at-risk kids and youth violence. Not all will work everywhere. Tastes vary. Needs vary. Results will vary. That's why there are choices.

Here are some of the choices in the "Coaching the Streets" menu:

MENTORING—A main course to be offered everywhere.

AFTER-SCHOOL PROGRAMS—For the danger hours after school lets out.

MUSIC—It fits the tastes of Memphis, the "Music City."

CUISINE—For New Orleans, a tasteful high school course.

MEDICAL MAGNET—It worked for a South Bend high school.

ALTERNATIVE SCHOOLS—Where the lost can find their way.

NEIGHBORHOOD WATCH—Neighbors looking out for their own neighborhood.

G.R.E.A.T.—A federal program offering a great alternative to gangs.

BAM—A Chicago-style program for "Becoming A Man."

COUNTERINSURGENCY—Springfield, Massachusetts, borrowed it from the military.

BASKETBALL—Keeps at-risk kids shooting on the court, not the streets.

SOCCER—Why not a soccer version of midnight basketball for Latino kids?

COLLEGE—College students help at-risk kids to pick education, avoid risk.

CORPORATIONS—They can choose to fund and promote programs that work.

JOBS—What employers need to provide for kids turning their lives around.

RICHARD "DIGGER" PHELPS, winningest men's basketball coach in the storied sports history of the University of Notre Dame, now is a college basketball analyst on ESPN. He is legendary as a coach for upsets of No. 1 ranked teams. In his 20 years of coaching at Notre Dame, his teams averaged nearly 20 wins a season and had a 100 percent graduation rate. After coaching, Phelps joined the administration of President George H.W. Bush to head Operation Weed and Seed, directing a coordinated attack on gangs, drugs and violence. He continues passionate interest in that cause, "coaching the streets" in efforts to stem youth violence and promote education opportunities of disadvantaged kids. Earlier books by Phelps include *Undertaker's Son*, an autobiography.

JACK COLWELL is a political columnist for The South Bend Tribune and on-line for Howey Politics Indiana. He has won numerous awards in newspaper writing and is a member of the Indiana Jounalism Hall of Fame. He frequently appears on television news and public affairs programs. Colwell is an adjunct associate professor at the University of Notre Dame, teaching journalism. He also collaborated with Digger Phelps in the writing of *Undertaker's Son*.